TOWARDS

AN ABIDING PEACE

THE MACMILLAN COMPANY
NEW YORK · BOSTON · CHICAGO · DALLAS
ATLANTA · SAN FRANCISCO

MACMILLAN AND CO., Limited
LONDON · BOMBAY · CALCUTTA · MADRAS
MELBOURNE

THE MACMILLAN COMPANY
OF CANADA, Limited
TORONTO

TOWARDS

AN
ABIDING
PEACE

R. M. MacIver

NEW YORK
THE MACMILLAN COMPANY
1943

CONTENTS

CHAPTER I

AN ABIDING PEACE?   I

CHAPTER II

THE PRICE OF PEACE   15

CHAPTER III

THE FOUNDATIONS OF ORDER   26

CHAPTER IV

THE SHORTEST WAY WITH DEFEATED ENEMIES   40

CHAPTER V

THE TERRITORIAL TERMS   52

CHAPTER VI

THE ECONOMIC TERMS   67

CHAPTER VII

THE TWILIGHT OF IMPERIALISM   88

v

Contents

CHAPTER VIII

THE GREATER CHARTER 102

CHAPTER IX

THE GREATER LAW 120

CHAPTER X

FRAMEWORK OF AN INTERNATIONAL ORDER 134

CHAPTER XI

PROSPECTS OF AN INTERNATIONAL ORDER 154

CHAPTER XII

DEMOCRACY AND THE FUTURE 167

CHAPTER XIII

THE PECULIAR ROLE OF THE UNITED STATES 183

TOWARDS

AN ABIDING PEACE

CHAPTER ONE

AN ABIDING PEACE?

I

Man is always at the parting of the ways. The peace that is to come will present some momentous alternatives. Abiding peace or a breathing spell between wars? Can we choose? There are those who say No. There are those who say Yes. There are those who would make the peace a longer armistice while the spent forces of war recover. There are those who would make the peace the beginning of a reign of peace.

Always we must choose anew which God we shall serve. The conditions of service are never clear. The best light of intelligence cannot pierce far into the mists. Always we take sides, for action cannot wait. So it has been since the first dim adventures of man. Always he must join his faith to his perception, and trust—not one or the other alone but both together. In some such combination of faith and perception this book is dedicated to the cause of an abiding peace.

Abiding peace—for some it is only a dream, and, as one of them said, "not even a beautiful dream". War, they say, is the judgment seat of men and peoples. In peace the peoples decay, in war they are reborn. War goes with virility and prowess and the heroic quality. War eats through the lethargy and enslavement of peace. War is natural, war is the divine ordinance. War is eternal. It has been with man from the first, it will be with him until the last. To think otherwise is to misread history. To believe otherwise is to be sentimentalist. The enfeebled, the effeminate, the craven, dread war and would impose on the universe their effete wishes and their futile hopes.

I

Even among those who dislike war there are some who still believe that humanity *needs* war, needs it as a moral or spiritual necessity. Even those who oppose war have sometimes felt, like William James, that we must find a "moral equivalent" for it. Many have been afraid of abiding peace. They have regarded war as the great challenge to creative effort, the nurse of invention, the spur of progress. They have held that war calls out the deepest loyalties and the finest powers of men, raising them beyond the petty concerns of everyday life, uniting them in a cause that mocks at death itself. These ideas have been developed into a philosophy of war by the military-minded men of all countries, though its most grandiose expression has been achieved by a line of German philosophers.

With this kind of philosophizing we shall not be concerned. We follow another road. It is a vain and endless task to counter an ethical philosophy on its own ground. Its ground is not the revelation of reality, or science. The evidences are innumerable and conflicting. An ethic can offer no proof that it is right, and we who oppose it can offer no *proof* that it is wrong. At best we can but controvert the "proofs" it offers. Take, for example, the claim that peoples become degenerate in peace and are regenerated by war. How impressive it sounds—and yet— Can history answer? Who has compared with scientific scruple the moral and spiritual conditions of the generations that have passed through the ordeal of war with the conditions of those generations that have escaped this "medicine of God"? Were the former generations and those which succeeded them morally and spiritually finer? The Greeks after the Peloponnesian War? The Central Europeans after the Hundred Years War? The French after the Napoleonic, and the British after the First World War? And again, were the succeeding generations, when the war was absent, morally and spiritually enfeebled? The Japanese during the long peaceful Shogunate? The British at the end of the nineteenth century? The American people before 1917? Merely to ask these questions is to show how far from scientific are the grounds on which rests the claim of the regenerative influence of war. It is not history, it is not science, that leads men to such valuations.

It may well be that men and nations need continually to be shaken out of the complacency of their settled ways. But is it war alone, or war most frequently, that fulfils this function? The ever-changing lot of mortal man has in it the potency of endless challenge. Always within it there arise disturbers and disturbances of the kind of "peace" that is inertia or complacency or the rusting of the spiritual armor. It is very doubtful that we need even a moral *substitute* for war.

Men have counted the number of wars in each century since historical records began. They have counted the number of years in each century that each country has been at war. On the average each of the greater countries has been in a state of warfare more than half the total time. They have counted the number of years that peace treaties have lasted. On the average they have lasted about two years. From such data they have concluded that warfare is the habitual condition of mankind. From the statistics of the past they predict the future. This method, superficial as it is, might serve if we were dealing with the weather or something else outside human control. But inside human society the projection of statistical rates or trends is nearly worthless. Two centuries ago we would have concluded from the same mode of reasoning that the majority of human beings would always live under rural conditions. A hundred years ago we would have concluded that the "expectation of life" at birth would never exceed forty years. A hundred years ago we would have concluded that slavery would always exist. Fifty years ago we would have concluded that men would never fly through the air. The mechanical counting of past occurrences will never yield us the secrets of the future.

They tell us also that war has many causes and will continue so long as these causes exist. This argument is no less faulty. The resort to war is the resort to a method of settling disputes between states. It may be a dispute over territory or over trade or over "honor" or over anything else. There are countless sources of dispute between the vast concerns we call states. But it is a misuse of language to call the causes of dispute the causes of war. They are causes of war only if war is an accepted mode of settling them. The causes of an instrument or agency—or rather of the resort to that instrument or agency—are not the uses made of it. It is just as absurd to call these disputes the causes of war as to call them the causes of guns. A human contrivance of any kind has no "cause" for existence—only a reason —and it has no reason for existence except the desire or the intention to use it. War has no "cause" except the intention of governments, under whatever conditions, to resort to war. War is "an instrument of national policy", and if men should decide to abandon this instrument the alleged causes could forever exist without producing the alleged consequence.

Disputes are inherent in human life—they exist wherever life of any kind exists. Man is a restless and pugnacious animal. He is never content. He is always a fighter, so long as his body nourishes the energy to strive. He fights for himself, for his family, for his group, for his party, for his faith, for his country —in short, for everything he prizes. And he is so endlessly variable, man from man, group from group, that difference and the strife of difference exist everywhere. We are not concerned with the fact that man is a fighting animal. We are concerned with one mode of fighting, on one level of organization. This mode itself has changed enormously, in its character and in its consequences. The reason why it is likely to be discarded is that man is a thinking animal, reckoning consequences, as well as a fighting one. It is fairly clear that the majority of men, under modern conditions, dread war—probably the vast majority. Why then are they drawn into wars? Not because some instinct compels them. Only because they have not learned, only because they feel powerless, to prevent wars. They have not learned because human organizing abilities have been stopped at the line where states have their boundaries.

What prevents an advance beyond this line? Man is an organizing as well as a fighting animal. At this line he has been stopped, not by any necessity in things but by traditions and prejudices and fictions about the state, and more particularly by an entrenched prejudice concerning a mystical thing called sovereignty. Nevertheless modern war is so destructive of his property and his happiness, so unpredictable, so deadly, so omnipresent, and so world-embracing, that it is surely no outrageous opinion to hold that his needs will in time get the better of his prejudices.

How long it will take we cannot surmise. It might happen very soon. It could happen even after the Second World War. That it *will* happen this writer is as certain as of anything not yet disclosed—and he has no such assurance about any other human development. He knows that this belief marks him a sentimentalist but he is not sentimental enough to fear that opprobrium. He is aware that learned historians and philosophers and geopoliticians and empirics of every kind pour scorn upon this belief. He holds it none the less, believing also that these "realists" misjudge the past, the present, and the future.

It is scarcely open to doubt that the people of England and the people of France and the people of Italy and the people of the United States did not *want* this war. There was no imperious urge within them driving them to war, no eagerness to fight, no longing for any spoils it might bring. It is highly probable that a considerable majority of the people of Germany and of the people of Japan did not *want* this war. It is doubtful whether any amount of indoctrination would have led the people of Germany to choose war, had they not been spurred by resentments and humiliations arising out of the First World War. The average man does not think in terms of power and world dominion. He moves in his own little circle. His everyday hopes and fears are utterly different from those that congregate around the seats of the mighty. The great majority of men are struggling for the means to live, for the few extra dollars that will save them from distress, insufficiency, or bankruptcy. The difference between the minute sums that mean so much to them and the prodigious billions that war costs is also a measure of the difference between their attitudes and those of the geopoliticians and the masters of men who cast up the reckoning of war.

The people think in other terms. To prepare them for war-like activities they need much indoctrination. They can be made warlike if they think their country is menaced or has been maltreated. Hitler fanned the flame of resentment among his countrymen. He could not have succeeded had not the victors of the earlier war prepared the soil for the seeds he sowed. The people of Germany had passed from defeat to unemployment and new privation, through inflation and vast insecurity. Their earthly god, their fatherland, had suffered mutilation, and they had suffered with it. They were ready to ingest the poison of warlike indoctrination. If we seek to make an enduring peace we must not disrupt the souls of men so that they fall easy victims to a deadly disease.

2

"Blessed are the peacemakers." But not always the peace-treatymakers. For the peace-treatymakers are often, even if unwittingly, the next-warmakers. No generation has arisen, or will arise, to call down blessing on the treatymakers of Versailles. Of the greater statesmen who made that treaty only one cared about an enduring peace, and he was baffled and distracted, and in the end resorted to compromise that possibly boded worse for his cause than would have been its complete rejection.

Of the other three one, Clemenceau, "the tiger", was senilely intent upon revenge; another, Lloyd George, was still cultivating the mass emotions; the third, Orlando, was a political trimmer lacking both authority and vision. Back of these men were the confused clamors of peoples weary to death of war but still carrying the mentality of war into their thoughts of peace.

"Blessed are the peacemakers." But not the appeasers. Not the Lavals, the Tisos, the Quislings. Not the compromisers. Not those who yield themselves to the lords of war. They feed the lust of conquest. They help the warmakers to realize their dreams. They are enemies of peace, because they willingly accept the servitude that the warmakers love to impose.

"Blessed are the peacemakers." But not the isolationists. Not those who wash their hands in innocence when the world is torn by war. Not those who stand apart and merely pray vain prayers that war shall cease. In so doing they are aiding the warmakers. They make it easier for the warmakers to achieve their goals. There are no sidelines in modern war. It enters every home in every land. Those who do not work and fight, however they can, to end the power of warmakers are not the friends, but the foes of peace.

"Blessed are the peacemakers." But these are not the passive resisters. We should respect their conscience and their hatred of war. But the individualist attitude of passive resistance does nothing to end war. Military aggression, the rule of force, is not defeated by passive resistance. War inevitably engulfs whole peoples—once it is begun. Once it is begun there is only victory and defeat. The conscience of the individual cannot change that law.

Who then are the peacemakers? Surely those, and those alone, who devote their will, their heart, and their strength to the purpose of establishing the dynamic reign of peace; who face the difficulties, perplexing though they be, of the reorientation of human attitudes that the reign of peace presupposes; and who are undaunted by these difficulties, alike because they know that war has become intolerable under the conditions of our civilization and because they believe that mankind has the continuing power to remake its institutions according to its needs.

The crucial battle of the peacemaker is fought when the time comes to draw up the terms of peace. He must prepare for that final battle even while war rages. He must do all he can to influence in advance the peace-treatymakers. When war ends all men are filled with the deep yearning for peace, but most men are filled also with the passions, the animosities, the tensions, and the embitterments that war evokes. These emotions endanger the peace. Back of these lie certain traditional attitudes that stand in the way of abiding peace, the attitudes that perpetuate the existing order—or disorder—out of which wars arise. The peoples want an abiding peace, but they must be taught its conditions. The peoples want an abiding peace, but they must be ready to accept its conditions.

War is still a political institution, an accepted instrument of national policy, "the continuation of politics by other means", as it was quite properly defined by the German militarist, Karl von Clausewitz. What we have to do is to deinstitutionalize war. This means that we must build a new set of institutions and at the same time demolish an old set. We must abolish the independent sovereignty of the state with respect to other states, and we must organize an international system. Conditions, as we shall show later, are already ripe. It has become intolerable, in fact entirely ridiculous, that every few years some incident in the relations of two states should threaten the well-being of the whole world. No threats of war arise between New York State and Pennsylvania; no incidents precipitate war between the Italian and the French cantons of Switzerland. We must create an order in which wars are hardly less likely to occur between Germany and England or between Japan and the United States. We must create an order in which international war will be as anomalous as civil war—no longer the established fashion of settling the final differences between states, but at most a rare outbreak, like an earthquake in a world whose foundations are for the most part secure.

Of course it is not easy to build this order. How should it be? What great change in human institutions has been? Nevertheless nothing resists the will to change our institutions except the unwillingness to change them. And there are mighty persuasions that more and more are reinforcing the will to destroy this particular institution, until, sooner or later, it must be destroyed.

The forces of change inherent in human society can not be stayed by old-established institutions. Authority changes its dwelling place. The mighty are dethroned and the weak are raised to power. The process never ends. The inventiveness of man cooperates with the law of his mortality. The new generations tread upon the old. The new energies break the old moulds. Values and creeds are in motion and refuse to be imprisoned within their own traditions. The *status quo* is always on the defensive and always loses in the longer struggle. War is but a symptom of the endless struggle—neither its source nor its necessary means.

There is, however, one kind of social fixity that might most plausibly be held to require the solvent of war. The great changes of political frontiers have in the past been eminently determined by warfare. The surging life of peoples, the transformation of sovereignties, the growing and changing consciousness of national unities, the rise of new solidarities and the decline of old ones, the shifting of the foci of control are forever being manifested. But hitherto the ferment and dynamism of the changing state have registered themselves, have found expression or fulfilment through war-changed frontiers. Since, then, the expansion and contraction of states have hitherto depended—apart from the discovery and exploitation of new lands—upon the issue of wars it might be claimed that without the resort to war the political map of the world would be eternally static, and that an intolerable clamp would thus be imposed upon the changes rendered imperative by the vital energies of the more vigorous peoples, while the peoples rich in territorial possessions would retain, no matter what decline they suffered, the dominion won by their more virile ancestors.

But this contention ascribes to war a service that is necessary only so long as war itself governs the relations between states. In a world not regulated by war there would be no conquerors and no conquered. There would be no peoples struggling for the freedom to rule themselves, no oppressed minorities struggling for the right to join their compatriots, no sheer exploitation by alien powers over any part of the earth. Under such conditions, within the framework of an international order, the greater forces of change would still have their way. They would proceed more spontaneously than ever before, for the conservative barriers of entrenched force would no longer resist them. The creative culture of every area, large or small, would have freer play. The challenge of the new against the old would still sustain the endless drama of human life. This world order would be no utopia. It would have its recurrent crises, its insistent problems. Every age must find with travail and sweat its own solutions. If we solve the problem of war, if we discard this ancient instrument that is so ill fitted for the different civilization we have built, new problems will arise that lie beyond our present dreams.

3

There is a deeper reason why we need not regard the institution of war as eternal.

Wars are waged between peoples or communities. They are waged across frontiers, and the frontier divides people from people, community from community. No matter what other dividing line the champions of either side proclaim, whether race or religion or economic doctrine or political ideology or whatever else, it is always communities that are opposed in war. Each belligerent must fight and must suffer, must win or must lose, as a total community. This truth has greater significance

than ever before with the modern development of total warfare; the country as a whole is in the fighting line.

The logic of total war requires that communities be separate
as wholes. In other words, *without separateness war loses its
rationale.* Without separateness you are destroying your own
good, your own heritage, your own wealth, in the very act of
destroying that of the enemy. But separateness belongs to the
primitive world. The further civilization advances, the less there
is of it. When tribe fought against tribe they were essentially
separate. They shared no common good. In the earlier days of
our own civilization countries were relatively separate. They
could discount whatever common good they shared. The country as community could still think of itself as separate. The
rationale of war still held. Today it is less and less possible to
think of nation-communities as separate. In a not distant to-
morrow it will, in all probability, be impossible.

An ironical consequence is that the causes that bring war into
being are rarely the causes for which men fight in war. The
causes are disputes over territory, over dominion, over economic rights, and so forth; but once the war is started the
immediate ground of dispute becomes a secondary issue or
disappears from view altogether. The war takes on the aspect
of a life-and-death struggle between nations, in which the whole
future of each is involved. And the decision at the end of the
war is never merely or mainly a decision over the initial dispute.
The process of modern war disregards the considerations of
policy for the settlement of which war is in the first instance
invoked. If war is indeed an "instrument of policy" it is the most
uncontrollable of instruments. In the last analysis men do not
fight to win some prize of war. It is not for this that they offer
their lives and accept the heaviest sacrifices of all that is dear
to them. Whatever discipline or whatever indoctrination sustains them, they fight because their country is endangered.

That is why it is harder for Americans to summon up the war

spirit than for peoples that have been traditionally at enmity. For Americans do not so easily conceive that their country is endangered. On the one hand they feel secure, perhaps too secure, in their country's strength; on the other, being the off-spring of many peoples, they lack that sense of antagonistic separation that has obsessed the nations of Europe. And that is also why America can and should play a peculiarly important part in the making of the peace. For an enduring peace is not possible unless in the making of it we surmount the passions and the obsessions that perpetuate the condition of war.

What lies back of man's readiness for war—however it be played upon and controlled by the ambitions and lusts of the warmakers—is the sense of his belonging in some one precious union with his fellows. It matters not whether the union is the kin or the tribe or the folk or the nation. These are but the historical loci of his devotion. If you take one from him he must find another. If his spirit transcends one it is to discover a greater union. If the inventions he develops makes one too narrow, so that he must accommodate his prejudices to the ef-fective existence of a larger community, he will in time build it and find therein the union he must have. Or if it proves too large for him, too remote, too impersonal, he will cling to a nearer community within it. Man always seeks, man always finds, his community.

But he may conceive it wrongly, through prejudice and in ignorance of its true nature. Within our present civilization no country is an exclusive unity of all the interests of its members. It is not merely that no people is self-sufficient, economically or spiritually—it is that the good of every people is bound with that of others in far-reaching and deep-reaching ways. In the first place the economic well-being of every people depends to a large extent on the well-being of other peoples. Beyond that, the social heritage of every people is sustained and en-riched by the contributions of other peoples. There is no closed system of art or science or philosophy or faith that is the exclusive possession of any nation, unless it be the false faith in such exclusive possessions. Just as there is no uniformity of interest or of faith among the members of a modern nation, so there is no self-containedness of the conditions of its well-being. A nation has its own history, its own tradition, its own achievements, its own frontiers, and therewith its own consciousness of its unity. These things are perverted by false doctrine into a separateness it does not possess, a separateness from other nations that has become under totalitarian indoctrination a most dangerous and even fatal dogma.

It is no accident that the doctrine of uniformity and separateness has been cultivated by the warmakers. They have always cultivated it but never before with the all-embracing fanatical zeal of our modern totalitarians. It is no accident, because you must cultivate separateness if you want to develop militarism. You cannot develop militarism if you believe in a common good and a common culture. If you believe in the common well-being of nations you cannot believe in the exclusive unity of the folk. Our modern totalitarians have been separatist in the manner of the most barbarous tribes. For them, their own frontiers are the limits of such humanity as they still admit. At their frontiers they block all the intercourse of peoples. Across certain main avenues of the city of Warsaw they have constructed a high concrete wall, in order to make a ghetto. Thus they dismember a city in the name of social separation, and thus too they seek to dismember a civilization, damming behind the walls of their blind egoism the creative and liberating forces of mankind.

"Enmity is the basis of the state's existence," cries one of their popular writers. "Nationhood," says another, "means the wrathful separation of nation from nation." It matters not to these "blind mouths" that there exist states, more stable than their own, that are not based on enmity and do not live by wrath-

ful separation.[1] The United States, for example, does not depend
on the political driving antagonism against other states that for
these philosophers is the very being of the state. But the truth
is not their interest. Heirs of historic hatreds, they reason only
in the murk of their passions. They are all the more vehement
because they must contradict the facts. They would kill all
truth that is not congenial to their passions. They must at the
same time reject all the processes of culture that have built
the modern world.

They would reduce community to its most primitive form.
But they cannot kill the forces that for centuries have been
breaking the separateness of nations, that have been undermin-
ing the rationale of war between nations. In vain they resist
these forces. At length these forces will destroy them.

In the last analysis it is not war that spurs man's sacrifice
and his devotion. It is not nation, it is not country. It is that
union with his fellows to which he is emotionally attuned,
whatever it may be, however constructed or even imagined.
It is not a question of man's selflessness any more than it is of
his selfishness. What is at work is the imperative urge, the
social instinct, to safeguard one's community. The community
changes, it expands, it is no longer walled, it is community
beyond community. As in the past man has learned to accommodate his sense of union to the changing social reality,
so he will surely learn again.

[1] "Blind mouths," the indignant term applied by Milton in *Lycidas* to
ecclesiastical guides who betray their trust. It so happens that both the writers
quoted above are clerics—one Catholic, one Lutheran.

CHAPTER TWO

THE PRICE OF PEACE

I

Do we want an enduring peace? Then we must be willing to pay the price. The price of victory does not cover the price of peace. Peace too must be won, and it would indeed be strange if so precious an achievement, unlike any other human achievement, fell without price into our hands. The winning of peace makes certain clear demands upon us. Are we prepared to meet them? We pay millions of lives and billions of dollars and countless tears for the chance of victory. Shall we offer nothing for the one great good that this victory makes possible, an abiding peace?

There are those who are ignorant of the price and those who are unwilling to pay it. There are the selfish ones who peer at their own narrow interests and will not raise their eyes, no matter what portents are in the sky. There are the intolerant ones who make their group or their nation the standard of humanity. There are the embittered ones who have suffered grievously in the war and cry for justice. There are the stupid ones who cannot think beyond the old traditions or the old catchwords—these reactionaries are unwittingly the greatest enemies of peace. For a genuine peace, so far from being passivity, is a revolutionary thing. A war like this latest war is a revelation of the need for a revolutionary change. Somewhere, in the ordering of human affairs, there was grave defect to permit so dreadful a catastrophe. The problem of peace is to discover where it lay and to remove it. Any other peace will be merely a cessation of warfare. But we cannot find and we cannot remove so grave a defect if we persist in certain old attitudes, in certain old notions and valuations that have hitherto governed a great sector of human relations.

Peace has, first and foremost, what for want of a better name we shall call a psychological price. Since peace means a reconstruction of the relations between men as organized in states, it means also a reformation of the attitudes of men. The mentality of warmaking is the precise opposite of the mentality of peacemaking. War is division, peace is the healing of division. War is reciprocal destruction, peace is reciprocal construction. War is nation against nation, peace is nation joined with nation. Peace is these things *if* it is genuine peace, if it is peace just as truly as war is war.

If we want this peace we must heal division. If we want peace we must join with other nations in peace, *with enemies no less than with allies*. Here is where the psychological price is demanded. Already, as they read these words, there are those who are saying: "This man is tender to our enemies. He is on their side. He is dangerous." Those who say so show that they are unwilling to pay the psychological price of peace. When we plan for peace we must abandon sides. We must think of the whole. If we want an abiding peace we must think in the terms of peace, no longer nation against nation, but nation joined with nation.

It is, if you care to put it so, a scientific problem. Assuming that an abiding peace is our goal we ask, simply and squarely: under what conditions can it be attained? Since such a peace requires the cooperative activity of states, whether they have been our friends or our enemies, we ask again: under what conditions can we win this cooperation? To answer this question we must consider, among other things, how the peoples of the defeated countries will react to the terms we impose. Now one of the commonest difficulties in the way of our ordinary human relations is our inability to put ourselves in the place of others, to understand how our behaving affects their behaving. We look mainly at one side of the relation, our own. This difficulty is intensified when the other party is or has been our enemy.

Moreover, the time for the making of peace is just the time when we are least in the mood to reflect on the later consequences of the treatment we mete to other peoples and especially to enemy peoples. For that is the time when at last, if we are victorious, we can give free vent to the cumulative pent-up passions provoked in us by all the furies of war. The discipline is released, the barriers are down. It has often been remarked that at the end of a war peoples experience a gross reaction. The supreme effort, the vast tension, the sacrifice and the spirit of sacrifice, are over. There is, very understandably, a swing away from the heroic complex, from the sense of the great and unifying cause. There is a tendency to the dissipation of the solidarity fostered by the necessity that war imposes. At such a time men are likely to be disinclined to face with resolution the difficult but all-important tasks that must then be done—and to pay the price of peace.

So in making a peace with a defeated nation the victors are most apt to disregard its needs, to brand it with inferiority, to subjugate it, to humiliate it. They do not ask: what effect will this have on the peace we make? They do not seek to understand the feelings of the humiliated people. They do not realize that after all the humiliated people are men and women just like the rest of us, and will react to such humiliation as we too would react. The French, for example, did not consider the repercussions that would follow when they sent Senegalese regiments into Germany as part of their army of occupation. They did not consider how the infliction of such needless wounds to the pride of a people would imperil still more the peace.

It is the old lesson that Shakespeare put into the mouth of Shylock in *The Merchant of Venice* when Shylock turned the tables and said: "I am a Jew. Hath not a Jew eyes? Hath not a Jew hands, organs, dimensions, senses, affections, passions?

Fed with the same food, hurt with the same weapons, subject to the same diseases, healed by the same means, warmed and cooled by the same winter and summer, as a Christian is? If you prick us do we not bleed? If you tickle us, do we not laugh? If you poison us, do we not die? And if you wrong us, shall we not revenge? If we are like you in the rest, we will resemble you in that." In the affairs of nations there is also this vicious circle of injury and revenge that can be broken only when we have the intelligence to make a genuine peace.

To make it we must understand how the other parties to the peace will react, not immediately but in the longer future. The best way is to ask how we ourselves would react to similar conditions. To many men the very idea of being treated as they would treat their defeated enemies is simply unthinkable. They evade thinking of it by talk about treating the enemy as the enemy deserves. We may answer again in the words of the great writer who understood the hearts of men. "Use every man after his desert, and who should 'scape whipping?" Who can judge what *a people* deserves? Such talk conceals our un-willingness to face the true problem of peace. It is the childish-ness of group egoism.

In saying so we are not minimizing or glossing over the intolerable wrongs that our main enemy in this war has com-mitted. We have unutterable loathing for the barbarous doc-trines he has proclaimed and for the brutal manner in which he has enforced them. We deal with that subject in its proper place. Here the point is that in the making of this peace we have to face tremendous alternatives, and we must choose between them. After two world wars, devastating beyond previous ex-perience, the opportunity is approaching when we can build at last an enduring peace. Shall we or shall we not seize the opportunity?

First we must set our attitudes right. It is simply a question of common sense. It is not utopian; it is immensely practical. War has become too deadly and too disruptive to be borne.

Most men fear it and hate it. But many have short-sighted thoughts about the thing they fear and hate. They think, for example, that if the enemy is properly punished, if he is disarmed and rendered powerless, then we shall be at last secure. They do not reckon with human nature—and the peace of 1919 has taught them nothing.

If you want an abiding peace you must be ready to curb revenge and hate. If you want an abiding peace you must not set up conditions that the vanquished nations will bitterly resent for generations to come. If you want an abiding peace you must put the welfare of the whole above the immediate advantage of the part.

These conditions are surely obvious to any one who reflects on the subject. Unfortunately it is a subject on which people have not been taught to reflect. What stands in the way of reflection is the simple ethnocentric character of national sentiment. Men are suffused with the sense of the superiority and prestige of their own nation—which would be all very well were it not that it betrays them into foolish notions about other nations. We display too often the attitude of the small boy who believes that nobody else's father is so strong and brave as his. If we win it is because we are finer fellows; if we lose it is because of the treachery of the enemy or because of his overpowering numbers or because our own leaders have betrayed us. If we win we thank God and exalt ourselves; if we lose we do not mention God but we put the blame on scapegoats. So Hitler did after the First World War. So after the victories of the Second he exclaimed: "The deeds of our soldiers will go down in history as the most glorious victory of all time. In humility we thank God for this blessing." [Proclamation of June 24, 1940.] Hitler has the small-boy attitude in its extremest measure. Most of us have it in some measure, if without the ruthless fury of the German dictator.

Now any statesman of intelligence, if he is negotiating a peace, must reckon with this ethnocentric emotion. He must ask how it will respond to this or that treatment. It is very powerful, endlessly persistent, rooted in the depths of human nature. This is because it conveys the sentiment of community, because it is an expression of the social instinct itself. So when we insult or humiliate or suppress it, there is a terrific reaction. In the making of peace we must beware of offending it. Treat as you will the misguided priests and the lying prophets of the tribal God, so long as you leave standing the ancient altars of the tribe.

And when it is our lot to make the peace we must not let *our* ethnocentrism blind us to either the needs or the reactions of other peoples. The new peace must be built on the equality of all peoples before the new law, the law of nations. The pride and prejudice we have displayed towards peoples of other color must be controlled, if we haven't the courage and the wisdom to abandon it altogether. We must realize, among other things, that the peoples of the Orient must become as free and undominated as the peoples of the West. For our own self-interest we must realize it; for they vastly outnumber us, and if we treat them otherwise they will soon learn, if they have not learned already, to "better the instruction".

In this connection it is well to remember two further points concerning the sense of community, especially as it finds expression in national sentiment. The first is that though men make great sacrifices for the sake of it the sense of community is no pure altruistic self-effacing emotion. It is still "human, all too human". Men are very ingenious in identifying their particular interests with the cause of their community. When their own interests change they are all too likely to discover that the good of the nation has changed in the same direction. A tragic instance was the manner in which many politicians of France and many of its large industrialists changed their attitude after the debacle of 1940 and embraced a program of co-operation with the Nazis to save their patrimonies and their skins. This instance leads up to the second point. The face of national sentiment that is turned towards other nations is peculiarly changeful. It can change overnight from detestation to admiration, or *vice-versa*. The appraisal is always relative, never intrinsic. Illustrations are hardly necessary—there have been so many in recent times. Witness the various reversals of sentiment that have occurred with respect to Russia, or the various changes of popular French sentiment with respect to Great Britain.

The reason we have dwelt on these two points is to show that there is no insuperable difficulty in the adaptation of national sentiment to changing conditions and changing needs. Show people the necessity, bring home to them the fact that to win an enduring peace they must change certain attitudes and renounce others—then they will pay the psychological price.

Perhaps in the last resort the only price is the psychological one. The economic benefits of assured peace are so great and so universal, as against the staggering costs of war, that probably even the munition makers, turning to other products instead, would profit by it. And certainly if there are special interests that fatten on war we cannot regard the ending of that state of things as a price of peace but rather as in itself a most desirable goal. It would indeed be ridiculous to think that the people as a whole pay any economic price for peace. But there is another kind of price that remains to be considered. We may call it the political price, though as we investigate it we shall see that here too the exaction is solely psychological, that what is required of us is again a certain change of attitude, a correction of an illusory tradition, rather than any more tangible costs.

There is an old notion concerning the nature of sovereignty that stands in the way. If we are to have an enduring peace we cannot allow every state, or any state, to act as though it were independent and absolute in determining its relation to other states.

At a certain stage in the history of Western civilization, particularly in the sixteenth century, a group of legalist thinkers developed the notion of sovereignty, though its origins go further back. In the sixteenth century it was developed to serve a particular purpose. It was a way of asserting the need for centralized authority in the transition from feudalism to the national state. It served that purpose, and that purpose is now spent; but as so often happens the notion survived its usefulness. It was a pragmatic concept parading as an exercise in pure reason. People came to believe that this notion of sovereignty expressed the very nature of things. So it has become a dangerous notion, one most ill-adapted to the needs of our age. We should apply common sense to it and strip it of its pretensions. Then we would soon discover that this legal concept of sovereignty, as applied to the relations of states, is an absurdity. For sovereignty is a claim of right as well as of power, and it is a claim of the right to use power without regard for the rights of other states. This kind of "right" is sheer irrationality.

What must be done about sovereinty? We have to amend the notion and change certain practices of states that appeal to the notion but have no rightful ground, since they depend solely on power falsely claiming to be right. We must accommodate the sovereignty of the state to the needs of men. The prevailing notion of sovereignty spreads a smoke-screen over the facts.

Sovereignty is simply the authority that is exercised by or in the name of the inclusive political organization, the authority that government commands. "There is no power on earth that can be compared with it," wrote the philosopher, Hobbes. That is true if properly understood. For in the modern world this authority alone has the final right of enforcement. It is invested with this final right where it is, and because it is, the final co-ordinating power over the affairs of men. Somewhere, if we are to have a system of law and order, there must be a final authority, beyond which there is no appeal. But here there are two points to remember. In the first place this authority can be, and often is, assigned to it by the people, which can set it up and pull it down and therefore can make it in turn responsible. In the second place this final authority is organized differently under different conditions, and its location depends on the form of political union. In a unitary state it is unicentered. In a federal state it is multicentered. Where states are not completely separate and independent, the more inclusive union maintains a last court of appeal concerning those issues that raise the question of their respective powers. Sovereignty requires a last court of appeal.

This simple fact has been magnified into a tremendous myth. A vast amount of grandiose nonsense has been written about sovereignty. It is presented as a sacrosanct mysterious power somehow residing in a superorganism called the state. In earlier times men were content to say it was ordained of God; but modern philosophers of the Hegelian school took over the notion and inflated sovereignty into a kind of transcendent will and power. This expansion of the myth has taken its most gross form in the imagination of the philosophers of totalitarianism. To them the state is not an organization to carry on the business of the everyday humans who are its members. It has a will that is not the will of these members or of the mere flesh-and-blood politicians who make laws and decrees. Sovereignty is a being supreme and ineffable. Awesome and inscrutable forces hover about it. The mere individual, as one Nazi exponent puts it, is "a serving member of one great organic structure that encompasses his existence, his life and his action. He is a point of intersection for the motions of these powers, elemental, higher, historical, supermundane, that after their own will consume his self and his essence." [Hans Bäcker, *Deutschland und das Abendland*, Jena, 1935.] The state is a high and holy thing, beyond the thoughts and purposes of common men. If it is thought of as an instrument at all it becomes, for the followers of *Mein Kampf*, the instrument of the blood and instinct of the race. To that function it is directed by the One, the Führer, who knows best, who is the divinely appointed agent for the fulfilment of that function.

All this is dogma in the service of power. Authority is what we make it, or what we suffer it to be. It is an institutional device. It has the prerogatives we assign to it, or accept under it. The dogma has no necessary relation to the fact. The theology of sovereignty contains a clause that sovereignty is unlimited. Every federal state refutes that clause. It contains another clause to the effect that sovereignty is omnicompetent, in other words that no human interests or activities are withdrawn from its range of control. Every written constitution refutes that clause. Sovereignty is what we make it, and it cannot be defined as though it were a phenomenon of nature, which we must take as we find it.

We are therefore perfectly justified in asking what kind, what range, and what organization of sovereignty is best adapted to the requirements of our civilization. As soon as we ask this question we must recognize that completely independent states, bound to other states by no obligations other than those they care to accept and only for as long as they care to accept them, are alike perilous to and incongruous with our modern civilization. For we live in an age in which a vast number of our interests and our activities are deeply affected by the behavior of other states than our own. Our interests, spiritual and intellectual as well as economic, are for the most part not bounded within the frontiers of a state. The state we belong to is not, and can never again be—unless we revert to some degenerate barbarism—a self-contained unity, a closed system. The traditional doctrine of sovereignty is a presumptuous denial of this truth.

We must give up the proud stubborn prejudice of independence, the historic prejudice of the independent state. We resent any foreign interference in *our* affairs—that is all very well, but we must ask once more: what then are *our* affairs?

Are they still our affairs alone if what we do about them directly and vitally affects the well-being of other peoples? No one proposes that an external power should have the right to interfere with our purely domestic policies or our particular way of life. But there is a sphere of interdependence of such great importance for all concerned that the only reasonable course is to assign it, with proper safeguards, to an international system of control. At present every state acts as though it had the right to determine its foreign policy solely in terms of its own presumptive interest.

It has neither the right nor the power. There is no right where there is no obligation, where there is no constituted society governed by inclusive law. Nor has the individual state really the power to settle such issues. If it exercises its power to this end it is most likely to incite opposing power, and there is no certainty whatever that it will then achieve its objective. What then is this absolute sovereignty that states still assert, without any ground of right and without any efficacy of enforcement?

It may hurt our pride to abjure this prejudice of the independent sovereign will—but what is that price compared with the gain? The hurt will not be to our unity or to our loyalty— and the greatest menace of our civilization will be removed. The dogma of absolute sovereignty is maintained at an incalculable cost to the well-being of us all. Is it not better to give it up, to pay the psychological price?

CHAPTER THREE

THE FOUNDATIONS OF ORDER

I

UNTIL the present there has been no international order. Such temporary balance as has from time to time existed has had no sure foundations. Most obviously the prime condition of peace is the establishment of an international order.

Without law there is no order and without community there is no law. Law need not be written down or imposed or administered by any authority; it may remain in the realm of custom. This is the way of law in the simpler societies, where there has been a small compact community to guard it. But in the more complex forms of society there must be established law, ordained and administered by appropriate authority. In the international sphere no law, properly so called, has hitherto existed, whether ordained or merely customary. What has passed for international law has been a set of conventions and partial temporary agreements lacking the validity and strength of law. Such customary rules as have been invoked have not been guarded by any coextensive community. Such agreements as have been made have not been administered and enforced by any authority. Consequently they have not been capable of performing the eminent function of law in its proper sense, that of settling disputes by taking the issue to some decisive arbitrament—outside the parties to the dispute.

Now and again certain "high contracting parties" called sovereign states have convened and agreed on rules to govern their common interests. Some of these rules have been of a temporary nature, subject to periodic reaffirmation; others have been made without time limit. Some of them have been as it were international rules of the road, for the convenience of traffic—but without a policeman at the intersections. Others have been rules to settle controversial questions, but without any assurance that the "high contracting parties" would continue to abide by the settlement. Most of the minor rules have been very convenient for all concerned and have been rather faithfully observed; most of the major rules have been violated without scruple, though some states have been much greater offenders than others.

The main point, however, is that these rules have had no effective sanction. Moreover, the great powers have usually reserved certain issues as "non-justiciable", and these have been the very issues that most directly lead to war. Even when such powers have formally renounced the resort to war for the settlement of any issues, as in the Pact of Paris, their declarations have been detached from any realistic means of giving them effect. If the League of Nations had been born under a more favorable star, it might perhaps have built in time an international order. But for reasons we need not here discuss the League passed from modest efficacy in relatively minor matters to complete impotence in the face of crisis.

The fatal defect of the "international law" that has hitherto existed is most fully revealed by the fact that a large part of the "code" is devoted to the elaboration of the rules of warfare. What kind of a law is this that solemnly sets out the etiquette of law-breaking? No doubt even in war there may be a remnant of civilized usage accepted by the belligerents. But war, since its office is sheer destruction, must of its essential nature deny to the enemy nearly everything that humanity prizes. What then remains for the "international law" of war? It rests on the assumption that there is a vestige of community still uniting the belligerents. It rests on the further assumption that war can be limited by certain humanitarian considerations. As one international law authority puts it: "Unable to regulate the resort to war, international law did continue the ancient process of regulating the manner in which it was to be conducted."

The whole business of attempting to "regulate" warfare might be fundamentally challenged. If the objective in war is to destroy the enemy, what logic is there in regulating the mode of destruction? Is a state at war likely to submit to the disaster of defeat, with the concomitant annihilation of its soldiers and devastation of its territory, when it can prevent that catastrophe by resorting to a mode of warfare prohibited by a toothless "law"? Even laws properly so called are, as the Romans put it, "silent in the clash of arms". If we appeal instead to humanitarian considerations, what fine distinctions between the cruelty and pain of different kinds of violent death can be persuasive when the final alternatives of destroying and of being destroyed are weighed?

There are of course certain usages of warfare that belligerents on the whole respect—because and in so far as these usages do not seriously interfere with the primary objective of war, the annihilation of the armed forces of the enemy. There are rules regarding war prisoners, non-combatants, unfortified places, the white flag, and so forth—but the desperation of war unleashes forces that cannot be restrained within set limits. There are some practices that belligerents abjure, such as the use of poisoned weapons and of dum-dum bullets, but it would be rash to claim that they do so out of regard for "international law", since they have good reason to fear that the effect on the morale of their own troops of reprisals in kind would not justify the relatively slight immediate advantage of such practices. The failure to use poison gas in the present war must be explained in a similar way, since "international law" was no barrier to its use in the previous great conflict.

All the branches of the "international law" of war suffer from the same sickness. Take, for example, the articles adopted by the Second Hague Convention regarding the commencement of hostilities. These prescribe a formal declaration of war and a notification to neutral powers. But Japan attacked China without any declaration of this sort and it attacked the United States before it announced a state of war. Germany has repeatedly acted in the same manner. Or take the articles dealing with the rights of neutrals. The military imperative has overridden these rights, and the very concept of neutrality has been confounded.

The sickness of "international law" is not confined to its specific branches, it permeates to the roots of the system. So long as the only sovereign authority is the individual state, "international law" can be no more than a group of conventions exposed at every point to the law-ignoring necessities of the ultimate violence of war. *So long as "international law" is largely occupied with the "regulation" of war, there can be no international law deserving the name.*

Let us return to our starting point. The foundations of order are law and community. Without community no law is accepted and no code evolves. Without law there is no security, no established right or obligation, no refuge from the violence of overbearing force. So long as the recognition of community stops at the borders of states, so long must law be impotent to pass these borders. If we want an abiding peace we must build an international community. It is a vast task and the building will take a long time. But we can lay the cornerstone after this war, and we can set up an organization to continue the job of construction.

We must not be deterred by the fears of reactionaries who bid us go back to the old ways and conjure up lying pictures of a denationalized world in which our most precious possessions are the spoil of every outsider, in which the boundaries of nations are obliterated and no people is master in its own land. Within the greater order the heritage of every people will be far more secure than it has ever been before. Apart from this greater order the heritage of every people will be subject to worse menaces than it has ever been before. The inherent processes of change cannot be stayed by our fears or by our hopes. These processes make the lack of an international order an always deadlier danger. We cannot recover the past. If we do not achieve something better than its best we shall suffer something yet worse than its worst. The shadows of world-ranging wings fall upon the peoples. They herald fathomless terror and unlimited destruction, unless the dove of peace flies with them. Anyone who ridicules the sincere attempt to build an international order is far more profoundly fool than knave.

An abiding peace will mean the gradual creation of law to govern the relationships of states. Such law can arise only with the effective recognition of the common interests that bind the various peoples of the earth. The excesses of nationalism have prevented that recognition, but these excesses have always been fostered by wars and the threats of war. A greater assurance of peace would spread the recognition of the greater interests that have no national frontiers. It is a primary interest of all peoples that disputes between states should be settled by law, not by force. Power is the prize of the few, no matter how the many may be indoctrinated to support their ambitions. Welfare is the goal of the many, and historically its greatest obstacle has been the destructive ambitions of power. That is why the peace we make must be not merely a treaty between governments but a genuine peace of the peoples.

If it is to be a peace of the peoples it must not be a peace of the generals. The proper function of the generals is the making of war, not the making of peace. They cannot avoid reckoning in the terms of power. They cannot think of peace except in the language of strategy; they would contrive it so as to give the victors a commanding advantage against the next war. When the war is over, let us give the generals honors and monuments and a place in the history books—anything they ask except a voice in the peace. The politics of power, *Machtpolitik*, has been the curse of Europe. The traditional foreign policy of European countries has calculated alliances and balances of power, the seizure of immediate advantage, the out-matching and forestalling of contrary powers. It has, even on its own ground, invariably miscalculated. If it has had temporary successes it has always been wrong in the longer run. At the beginning of the twentieth century the British sought to achieve a "balance of power" against Germany. The calculation went astray. At the Versailles peace table the victors contrived a great preponderance of power against Germany. Their plans miscarried. After Hitler came to power the German militarists elaborately calculated the advantages of friendship with England in a war against Russia *versus* the advantages of friendship with Russia in a war against England. This plan miscarried. So it has been all through history. The calculators of force always miscalculate the relation between force and other things. One thing they always fail to calculate is the animating will of the peoples. They calculate forces but they know nothing of the forces that make history. They calculate and the peoples suffer. They calculate and the youth of the nations is consumed.

The spirit of America—not only that of the United States but that of all America, North and South—has been alien to this fatal obsession of the balance of power. It should be the special role of America to make certain that calculations of future strategy—the stock in trade of generals and traditional diplomats and of all the "realists" and geopoliticians who follow in their train—shall be banned from the next peace table. Thus only can we make a genuine peace of the peoples.

The League of Nations was at best a league of governments and not of peoples. The plan was nobly conceived but badly executed. The result was not a federation of nations. It lacked authority because it lacked the source of authority, the animating will of the peoples. Nevertheless the mere tentative of a league of nations was a landmark in history. Its foundations were insecure, and it fell. The old League of Nations was dominated by the governments of the victorious nations; it postulated a *status quo* attained through dominance. It was unhappily associated with a vicious and short-sighted peace treaty. In everything men first fail—and try anew. The need spurs the attempt. In the reformation of human institutions the strong consciousness of need at length achieves its goal.

2

The values of militarism—power, dominion, glory, conquest, spoliation—are all in conflict with the deeper values of human life. If a state is organized for war, it must suppress these profounder and more enduring values. The values of militarism are all relative. Power is as hungry with much as with little—as hungry for more and as dissatisfied with what it has. Power forever seeks what lies beyond the frontier, no matter where the frontier may be. Alexander weeps when there are no more worlds to conquer, and has no tears for anything besides. The conqueror enslaves new peoples and is no happier than before— but the misery of the enslaved, unlike the triumph of the conqueror, is not illusory.

To make an enduring peace we must, so far as in us lies, set up policies that are the direct negation of militarist policies. We can see this clearly if we consider the policies of the fascist states. Fascism, especially in the Nazi improvement of that system, is man oriented towards war. The Nazis, true to form, have shown a remarkable thoroughness in carrying that orientation into every department of human life. If man is to be oriented towards peace we must reverse the Nazi policies in every department.

What fascism divides we must unite. What it rejects we must embrace. What it denies we must affirm. What it affirms we must deny. *The principles that fascism flouts are precisely the principles on which a world order must be founded.* We must make power responsible—fascism destroys the responsibility of power. We must set the law above the edict—fascism has turned edicts into laws. We must make justice universal—fascism has made it the prerogative of party. We must liberate minorities and assure them rights as absolute as those of majorities—fascism has suppressed minorities and made rights the exclusive possession of its adherents. We must abolish, to the utmost, racial discrimination—fascism has made it gospel. We must assure that the free expression of opinion determines political change—the primary act of fascism is to suppress free opinion. We must protect the free organization of social groups—fascism rules it out. We must detach the cultural life of man, his creeds, his arts, his final values, his individuality, from the police power—fascism has straitjacketed human life. We must give labor the fullest rights of organization—fascism has everywhere denounced these rights. We must make the state the servant and agent of the people—fascism has everywhere made it the master.

These anti-fascist democratic principles must be made the charter of the coming international order. Only on the basis of these principles can an international order be established. For fascism is man oriented towards war, and democracy, in its fuller development, is man oriented towards peace. The institutions we erect to safeguard the international order must embody and promote these principles.

Here, however, a distinction is necessary. It is highly important that all states should be enlisted in the international order, since an international order must be also a world order. No states that are willing to join should be excluded, as was done at the founding of the League of Nations. The prestige, resources and power of the United Nations will assure in the hour of victory the enlistment of virtually all neutral states. If any disaffected state should remain outside, practical considerations would soon induce a change of attitude. As for the defeated states, the terms of peace should require their inclusion in the international system. We assume, then, the adherence of all states to the confederation of peace. But all states are not ripe for democratic institutions. The attempt to impose democracy would be foolish and abortive. We must not forget that the greater part of the earth has never known democracy, even on the most lenient interpretation of that term. Democracy must grow, not be imposed. It must evolve from the effective will of the peoples.

There are good reasons for believing that it would so evolve under a regime of abiding peace. What, then, should be required of the adhering states is that they renounce certain principles of fascism, particularly those destructive of minority rights and of cultural liberties—a subject we shall later discuss in detail—and that they accept the charter of democratic freedom as a goal to be pursued by all states. This requirement would be, on the whole, readily accepted, since practically all states, outside the enemy countries, pay at least lip service to democracy and we must trust that time and peace will gradually turn profession into practice. Our most powerful non-democratic ally, Soviet Russia, has been profuse in its proclamations of democracy. Our other great non-democratic ally, China, has for the most part, throughout its long history, exhibited to the highest degree the essential democratic virtue of the toleration of differences, and its leading statesmen have in recent times exhibited strong sympathies for the democratic system. There is therefore no doubt that the charter of the international order would be readily approved. The institutions set up for the regulation of international affairs would themselves exercise a powerful influence in the further evolution and expansion of democracy. That is all we can ask for, and that is enough.

3

The institutions of the international order would promote and shelter the growth alike of international community and of international law.

The conditions favorable to the sense of an international community already exist and are forever being advanced by the economic and cultural interdependence that is stimulated by the progress of technology. Political considerations and nationalistic sentiments block at many points the development of a greater enriching interdependence. They erect barriers—spiritual and economic barriers—at every frontier. Were the menace of war removed these inhibiting forces would lose much of their power. The sentimental arguments for national self-containedness, or autarchy, would be deprived of the strong support of militarist fears, and the selfish interests of the few would find it harder to oppose the common interests of all. Community would tend to find its natural range, the range of the values for which and by which men live. The greater international community would enclose the nearer and dearer communities to which men belong. These nearer and dearer communities would not be lost in the greater. Even in the closest federation the nearer communities do not lose their distinctive character, as the experience of Switzerland and of the United States reveals. New England and the South, the Kentucky Mountains and New York City, are as distinctive and different as the most ardent regionalist would want them to be. The sense of community and the range of community do not depend, except artificially, on the artificial barriers we set up. They depend on the social nature of man as he adapts himself to the various environments within which he lives.

The differences between human groups would not be submerged. The ways of life, the mores characteristic of different groups, would not lose their appeal. Each group would be no less able than before to retain its identity, for one great source of intolerance would now be removed. Each nation would be not less able to cultivate its preferred ways of life, for it would be autonomous in its proper domain. There would still be the endless conflicting and competing claims of group values and interests. Strife and struggle would persist, for better and for worse, in myriad forms. But they would also remain within the enclosing community, without the brutal and irrelevant resort to lawless force to stimulate, intensify, and embitter the prejudices everywhere natural to mankind.

The growing recognition of the greater community would

in turn be confirmed by the growth of the greater law, the law of nations. At last this long-desiderated form of law, the law interpreted by an international tribunal for the settlement of disputes between nations, would reach the full status of law. What does this mean? It means that disputes between nations and nation-groups would be referred to a recognized authority, set up and accepted for this purpose. Thus a genuine system of public international law would in time be evolved.

An established authority implies the assurance that its decisions are binding. There is no authority, and there is emphatically no law, if the judgment of the court is of no effect apart from the willingness of the litigants to comply with the judgment. Law may be violated, but there is no law unless acceptance is the rule and unless violation is subject to the sanction of the law. There are various ways in which the sanction operates, according to the kind of law. The law of the church has a different sanction from the law of the state. Constitutional law has a different sanction from statute law. Each kind of law has a sanction appropriate to its type. What then must be the sanction of international law?

Let us insist again that the lack of sanction has hitherto made what has passed under the name of international law a frail and ineffective thing. During the attack of Italy on Ethiopia the League of Nations made a half-hearted attempt to employ economic "sanctions," without avail. But the authority of the League was insubstantial. A greater, more representative, and better founded organization was needed, the guardian of a genuine law of nations. Here we again face the question: what sanction can, what sanction must, attach to international law?

There is much division of opinion on this question. There are those who believe in international law but say it should not, and need not, be backed by force. We strongly assert the contrary position—*there will be no international law, as true law, until the regulations of an international authority are capable of being, at need, enforced.*

Let us remember that the one power on earth that in modern times has possessed the prerogative to exert its own force without incurring the sanction of law, in order to gain its own will, is the state. Let us remember that so long as this prerogative holds there can be no established international order. Let us remember that to abolish this ancient and deeply entrenched prerogative of states drastic action is absolutely necessary, backed by the growing consensus of the peoples who hate war. Wishing and hoping and praying will not suffice. Let us remember that the threat of force cannot be removed without countervailing force. The threat of force between individuals is controlled by the delegated force of the community. The threat of force between nations can be controlled only by the delegated force of the community of communities, the representative international authority.

These are the alternatives: either states maintain air forces, armies, and navies to impose their respective wills by bloody warfare one against another—in which case there can be no international order—or else there cease to be military establishments maintained for this purpose by individual states. It is not the scale of armaments, but the very existence of them, that is at stake. Unless they are totally abolished, as the last "argument" of individual states, there can be no assurance whatever against war and the ruinous international anarchy that erupts in war.

So the question is narrowed to this point: if national armaments are abolished what kind of force, if any, do we need for the maintenance of international order? Some say none is necessary, or desirable, or anyhow practicable. Perhaps it is because they are quietists or pacifists—in a certain sense of that word. They find no place for force in their dream of a better world. Or it may be because they cannot conceive of an international force that could baulk the will of great national powers, and hope that other modes of peaceful persuasion would suffice.

No enduring social order rests solely, or even mainly, on

force. No enduring social order exists that is not somehow and somewhere protected by force, even if that force is latent most of the time. What we are talking of is protective force, police force. It lies back of all public law. It stays the hand of violence, of lawlessness. It protects the law-abiding. We dare not underrate this role of force. We are dependent upon it every day of our lives. It checks the upthrust of sheer violence that otherwise, under the impulsion of egocentric—or ethnocentric—passions, would first crack and finally rend the firmament of order.

An international police force would not dictate to any state what it should do or refrain from doing. It would merely be in reserve to uphold the law that states together, through their international instruments, have laid down and accepted. In a world no longer filled with armaments it would be a guarantee against piratical forces, against violent coups directed by groups that might take advantage of the reign of peace, against adventurers who might make incursions across the borders of their own states—as D'Annunzio did at Fiume. An international police force would be the symbol—the necessary symbol—of the greater will that sustains the greater law. It represents the ultimate limit in the economy of force, when the community of nations stretches to the ends of the earth.

The size, composition, character, training, and functions of such an international force will require careful determination, but we need not here deal with this particular problem. We need say only that the international police force is predicated on the understanding that the armaments of individual nations will be not merely reduced, but *entirely abolished*. The mere reduction of armaments guarantees nothing, offers no protection whatever against war or against future "armament races". The process of disarmament may for practical reasons be graduated but the plan should involve the complete disappearance of national armed forces (aside from police forces) within a specified term of years.[1] A thoroughly qualified international board should be set up to deal with the many problems involved in the execution of one of the most epoch-making changes in the organization of mankind.

There is one further point it is highly important to stress. We have been contemplating the formation of a world order—a development that is ultimately inevitable and that for the sake of our children and our children's children should be inaugurated in the hour of opportunity at the close of the war. But no imposed or constructed order can set bounds to the inherent and intrusive forces of change that are at work in human society. Instead, it must be responsive to these forces, if it is to abide at all. Man the inventor, the innovator, the group-maker, the rebel, the self-seeker, the visionary, is the restless unit of ever-changing group formations. The processes of change must not be banked by the formalism of established law. If we are to have a world system it must be flexible, responsive to a multitude of changes, changes in the equilibrium of population, in the production and distribution of wealth, in the foci of cultural and social dominance. The bottles must be renewed ere new wine is poured into them. But this is a problem we shall face in due course.

[1] At present the army acts as a reserve police force against tumult and insurrection, a function for which it is not particularly well adapted. A small mobile police formation, trained thoroughly in the duties and responsibilities of citizenship, should be provided instead.

CHAPTER FOUR

THE SHORTEST WAY WITH DEFEATED ENEMIES

I

PRESIDENT Wilson, addressing the Congress on the declaration of war with Germany, April 2, 1917, made the statement: "We have no quarrel with the German people." While we are fighting them we do have a quarrel, a tremendous quarrel, a life-and-death war, with the German people. Modern war engrosses and is fought by whole peoples. We fight not an army only but a people in arms. That is inevitable. But when the war ends we should end also our quarrel with the German people and other peoples we have fought. In this respect as in others we must achieve that most difficult thing, a reversal of our attitudes. To conduct a war a peaceful people must reverse its attitudes: a peace-loving people must again reverse them to make a worthy peace. During war we must give up many of the habits and the freedoms of democracy, and we must be ready to resume them when the war is over. We must give up the freedom to organize our business for our own profit, we must give up the freedom to strike, we must give up the freedom to play party politics. In the United States we were slow to adapt ourselves to the necessities of war. It seems, for example, almost incredible that in the black days after Pearl Harbor a representative from New York State should have raised in the House a petty charge against the Commander-in-Chief of the nation's forces to the effect that his son when ill had received some trifling favor from the army. Numerous other glaring instances might be adduced of the failure to realize what war means. The nation as a whole, though still with many exceptions, did at length adjust itself to the necessities of war. In turn it must learn the no less difficult and no less imperative adjustment to the necessities of peace. First among these imperatives is the recognition of how to treat the defeated enemy peoples.

The shortest way with defeated enemies is to take the sting out of their enmity. We are dealing with whole peoples, and peoples live forever, or at least for the kind of "forever" that alone has meaning for human beings. When we are dealing with individuals or with particular groups, ruling groups, interest groups, ideological groups, we may have to deal with them according to the difference between them and us. But when we are dealing with peoples we must deal with them according to the likeness between them and us. For peoples live on, and ruling groups and interest groups and ideological groups change and pass. Peoples live on in their common humanity.

The history of the government of man by man is a record of endless miscalculations, of policies that went wrong, of stratagems that failed, of short-lived triumphs that ended in disaster. Where long-lived success has been attained in the use of power, it has been mainly where cooperative principles have been accepted; where, for example, the disposer of power, like Julius Caesar and his successor Augustus, has the insight to offer an inclusive citizenship to the vanquished peoples. The historical record underscores the conclusion, no less revealed in the experience of our every-day affairs, that there is no greater source of miscalculation in the ordering of human relationships than the inability to understand the other party to the transaction, and particularly the failure to give sympathetic consideration to his genuine needs. For this reason the making of peace should be taken entirely out of the hands of the military. Let it be theirs to make war but never to make peace. Nor should the making of peace be entrusted to the "experts". We should go to them for information, not for policy; often, in matters involving human relationships, the most knowing and the most clever men make the most disastrous blunders. The primary need is understanding; the primary failure is not the lack of knowledge but the emotional block that prevents us from using our knowledge to comprehend the consequences of our projected policies.

If the Germans were to win this war they would impose a horrible peace. The ultimate vindication of our cause is that we shall seek a peace infinitely preferable and vastly more secure than that which our enemies would impose. Peace, to be secure, must be such that it is welcomed by all men of good will among all nations, by all who pray for good will among men, whether they have been our allies or our enemies. The unbalance of the ethnic or nationalistic outlook is nowhere so tragically displayed as in much of the talk about the coming peace.

They say: "Keep the enemy down, keep your heel on his chest so that he will not rise again and fight." They say: "Treat him as he treats others. The only treatment he understands is the kind he gives, the whip and the muzzle." They say: "The enemy must be punished for all the wrongs he has done, punished so severely that he will learn the lesson and be deterred by fear from breaking the peace again." But this is loose and dangerous thinking. Whom do you punish? Those who were actually responsible for terrible outrages? Very good, so far as you can discover them. By all means let us punish them. But the people as a whole? The growing generation too? Will it be to them a just punishment for crimes? Will it not be to them, quite inevitably, quite humanly, a cruel oppression to stir up fierce resentments and the burning desire for revenge? So the dreadful cycle is again prepared.

Suppose, in your ignorance of human psychology, you propose to punish the present adult population of the enemy countries, attributing to them the guilt of the war? But that is vain, for it is not they who will engineer the wars of the future. And have they not already endured the worst of punishments, the punishment that war itself, bereft of all triumphs and spoils, inflicts on a people? If you must think in terms of guilt and punishment, what more punishment do you require of them than the destruction of their finest manhood, the tears of their women, the malnutrition of their children, the privation, the anxiety, the terror, the disruption, the whole inestimable toll of war? Shall we punish them more because we also have suffered these things? The adult generations do not need more punishment to be cured of any desire for war. And punishment is not the cure for the generations that come after.

If we think it is, we again make the fatal division of man into two orders of being, with entirely different springs of behavior, the one we belong to and the one our enemies belong to—the fatal division that has poisoned the Nazi soul, or made it Nazi. Any abiding peace must be based on the premise that all peoples respond in a similar way to similar treatment. There is no peace between the dominant and the dominated. There is no real peace between gaolers and prisoners, no matter what righteousness the gaolers proclaim. That way there is no end of war or of the spirit of war. This truth has been proclaimed by the great prophets, by Buddha, by Confucius, by Christ.

We have insisted on the need for a reversal of attitudes, but the need goes deeper than that. In the matter of international relations all peoples still behave, for the most part, like small children. Modern psychologists, such as Jean Piaget, have shown conclusively that the younger a child is the less does his behavior take into account the personality of those with whom he comes into contact. At first he is completely egocentric. Experience and indoctrination evoke in the growing individual an area of social comprehension, but it has many limitations and in particular it is bounded, for most men, by the frontiers of their state. They remain ethnocentric. They cannot comprehend other peoples as they can their own. In dealing with other peoples—not necessarily with individual members of other peoples whom they may happen to know but with other peoples as peoples—they still behave like small children. This attitude characterizes men in every station of life. They may be prominent statesmen or they may be great generals, but when they condemn alike all Germans or all Japanese, lumping them all together as people, as the wicked against the righteous, they still show in this respect the undeveloped mentality of childhood. They are in this respect not socially grown up. Once upon a time this ethnocentricity mattered relatively little. Other nations were remote. Science and technology had not yet bound the peoples of the world within a network of common interest. Now it matters enormously. Ethnocentric attitudes have brought the most pitiable ruin to the nations of the earth.

The President of the United States has reinforced the lesson. "The present great struggle," he said in his address of February 23, 1942, "has taught us increasingly that freedom of person and security of property anywhere in the world depend upon the security of the rights and obligations of liberty and justice everywhere in the world." In making peace we must realize that no country can be secure so long as any important country is seething in insecurity. The world is already too deeply committed to interdependence to admit this kind of disparity.

After the war we shall have to live in the same world with the German people, and we should treat them so that we can live together in peace. In war the principle must be: do to the enemy as he would do to you and do it first. In peace the eternal first principle of ethics stands as the condition of well-being, in the relations alike of men and of peoples: do to others as you would have others do to you.

The Germans are not a nation of devils. They are a nation of ordinary folk. They are a nation of patient industrious people, workers, farmers, professional men, petty officials, and all the rest. They are perhaps peculiarly docile before authority, and they are more easily regimented than some other peoples. They have the pride that every nation has in itself, a pride as unreflective and as spontaneous as that of any other people. They have enthroned a devil's philosophy, under conditions that gave the most dangerous and barbaric aspects of their cultural heritage supremacy over the pacific and decent aspects. The reasons are understandable to any intelligent student of mass psychology. Infinitely deplorable as are the results, the Germans are still men like other men. They are not cast in one mould, any more at least than the rest of us. They have exposed the most evil and brutal aspect of humanity—what people has not at some time in its history? They have also revealed some of the finest achievements of humanity—in poetry, in music, in art, in invention, in the quiet pleasures of everyday living.

It is true that in recent times they have nurtured the most ruthless militarists and the most sadistic oppressors. But these enemies of human progress millions of Germans have sought vainly to resist. Even at the height of the tension and terrorization, when the end of the ill-starred Weimar Republic was in sight, the Hitler party never won fifty per cent of the electorate. It is true that after the Hitler regime was set up a majority of the German people—though how large no man can say—approved the Nazi program. But indoctrination is powerful over all men, and let us never forget that even in our own country there were many who applauded Huey Long and there are today not a few who under far less provocative conditions have shown a readiness to wear a shirt that resembles the brown shirt and to follow a flag that differs little from the swastika.

Some people believe that we shall fight Germany more unitedly and more powerfully if we accept the "nation-of-devils" theory. This view is a profound mistake. We are most united in war when we are inspired by a great and noble cause, worthy of all our efforts and sacrifices. We have a greater cause if it embraces the strong hope of a better and happier world. Nothing less will compensate for the blood and tears, the toil and sweat. The hope of deliverance, of a new advance of humanity, is strengthened by the conviction that the war we fight can lead to an enduring peace. How can it be enduring if the Germans are not men like other men, capable of sharing with other men a better world? Let us consider the testimony of those who are thoroughly familiar with the German people. A former statesman and political scientist of Germany, a man who has every reason to detest Hitler and all his ways, writes as follows:

The current regime may have succeeded in educating a small "elite" to enjoy danger, violence, cruelty and the comparative stupidity of a life shaped permanently by external events, by commands and enforcements; but a vast majority of the people still prefer a life made calculable by law and order, and reasonable within the limits of one's own decisions. Strange though it seems it was precisely because of such a preference that millions of Germans accepted National Socialism. They believed its promises that a millennium of stability, prosperity, and security would follow what had been a long era of uncertainty and confusion. (Hans Simons, "Germany and a Democratic Order," in *The American Scholar*, Autumn, 1941.)

If we have doubts on this issue let us reflect that the view we take of the character of a people, inadequate and subject to bias as it always is, nevertheless is likely to be fairer under normal conditions of peaceful relations than it is amid the horror and devastation of a war they have inflicted upon us. Let us also recall that in the further past the Germans were not more warlike a people, indeed on the record were less devoted to war, than say the English or the French. If so, we are not confronted with a spirit so eternal that under a happier organization of the world it must still arise to block the road of human advance. Even the leader of the British school of thought that lays the blame squarely on the German people as a whole is willing to admit so much. "The soul of a people," says Baron Vansittart in his book, *Black Record—Germans Past and Present*, "can be changed. Other peoples have performed the feat. Why not Germany?"

The primary aim of a peace settlement, we again insist, should be to build for all peoples, enemies as well as friends, the conditions under which they can participate, whatever their differences may be, in the liberties and securities that all men seek to attain for themselves. Let us beware lest, in denying these to our enemies we are not in effect denying them to the coming generations of our own people. Those who call for ruthless suppression should try to understand the nemesis that so often has followed ruthless suppression. Those who would brand this plea as sentimentalism or even—God help us!—as secret sympathy with the purposes and policies of the enemy should try to realize that the unbridled passion of war is the worst guide for peace. Our passions are things of the day, but law stands inexorable, and not least the law of human nature.

"If you prick us do we not bleed? . . . and if you wrong us, shall we not revenge?"

2

Certain conclusions follow directly. Let us first look at the negative ones.

There must be no sweeping "indemnities," no colossal "reparations." No doubt it would be very gratifying, and very congenial to our sense of justice, if one could make the Germans and Japanese pay the cost of the war they brought upon us. But the world is not made that way. It is no use kicking against the pricks. We can of course make them disgorge all the recoverable treasures, works of art, and other enduring goods of which they have despoiled the conquered countries. Beyond that the vanquished can pay only in exportable goods. All they can pay is whatever surplus of exports over imports they can establish. If their economic systems are to function without dangerous or intolerable strains this surplus is necessarily very limited. At the first they will need our exports of foodstuffs and other necessaries to restore their exhausted economies. We shall have to feed our hungry enemies.

From the standpoint of our sheer self-interest it will be doubly advantageous for us to do so. It will reopen the fructifying channels of international trade, enabling at the same time our farmers and other producers of raw materials to clear their elevators and stock-piles of what will otherwise become in time a stagnating over-supply. At the same time it will herald the new world of more enduring peace. It will prevent the economic tensions and the embittered class conflicts that otherwise must prevail in the vanquished countries. It will help to remove the rankling motives for revenge that fester and breed secretly in a disorganized economy. If we follow a contrary policy we shall be giving support to the elements that hate us, to the forces that hate democracy, and they can very well become powerful again if in our shortsightedness we lend them this support.

At the close of the First World War the aftermath of the policy of making the enemy pay the major cost was clearly predicted by John Maynard Keynes, in his book entitled *The Economic Consequences of the Peace*. But the warning was not heeded until it was too late. The victors gained nothing and lost everything. Their wiser policies—the evacuation of the Ruhr, the Locarno Treaty, the scaling down of reparations—bore no fruit because the seeds planted by their earlier policies were already in strong growth. These wiser policies did not penetrate to the roots of the evil. The combination of economic privation, turned into disaster by the inflation, with national frustration and embitterment, rendered all-pervasive by the spectacle of a dismembered and alone disarmed country, could no longer be countered by such alleviations. The most dangerous elements flourished in the crisis. In a Germany seething in discontent the middle ground of liberalism could no longer be held against the "fell opposites" of communism and fascism. The Weimar Republic was overthrown. The time for reconciliation had been lost. Then, at length, "appeasement" became a hideous blunder, and then, at length, it was given full play by the victorious nations, inert in the face of, even unconscious of, the menace they had fostered.

It is said that experience teaches fools. On the contrary, the fools are those whom experience does not teach. It is our wisdom not to repeat the follies of the past. After terrible experience our opportunity to be wise will come again, and most of all in the treatment of our defeated enemies.

In this respect various proposals that have been given considerable endorsement must be summarily rejected. We should not, for example, try to impose internal democracy upon the vanquished. Democracy must grow from within, though we should encourage its growth. But if we impose it we do the same kind of thing as if we imposed a religion. We destroy its spirit and we give much aid and sustenance to its enemies. There are, it is true, certain features of totalitarianism that we must do our utmost to check; these will be dealt with in a later chapter. But we must otherwise leave each country, if we expect to have any genuine harmony, to determine its own form of government.

Another unwise proposal would have us send after the war a corps of "educators" to Germany, Italy, and Japan, to counteract the insistent and exclusive indoctrination to which their authoritarian governments have subjected youth. The proponents fear that if this is not done the deep imprint of ruthless and sustained propaganda will still control the attitudes of the generation now rising to manhood and recreate the peril through which our civilization will have passed. It is possible that the premises of this argument are mistaken. There is revulsion from as well as subjection to propaganda, and the former may be stronger when the indoctrination has been associated with the dreadful consequences of defeat. However this may be, assuredly the proposed remedy is worse than futile. It is another instance of the unilateral ethnocentric way of regarding other peoples. Imagine the situation in reverse. Suppose a phalanx of victorious Germans were to come to us, their defeated enemy, in the guise of educators and evangelists of the totalitarian way of life! Would that way be thereby endeared to us? Would we not find it all the more intolerable? Would it not stir our deepest resentment? If we wanted Germans, even those Germans who secretly chafe against the tyrannies of their system, to lose all sympathy for the democratic way of life, we could not find a more effective method.

For like reasons we should reject the proposal to set up after the war a world organization of the democratic, the more or less democratic, nations. Some people have championed what they vaguely call "a world organization of free peoples." This assemblage, by any definition, would be even more restricted than a "world organization" of the victorious nations, for some of these certainly could not be counted in the democratic category. Considerably more than half the world would not belong to this "world organization." What then could it be but an alliance of powers seeking to control the rest, thereby inevitably inciting a counter-alliance? So the world would again be divided into two camps, and the very name of democracy would become a sword of division. Thus the road to another war would be prepared, in which ideologies and power interests would be ranged against one another more surely than ever before. If we are to have a world organization—and we badly need one—it must embrace all nations, under a charter that guarantees a few absolutely fundamental rights but otherwise leaves every nation free to choose the kind of government it prefers. For the immediate reconstruction period after the war there will of course have to be set up a control organization dominated by the victorious nations, but it should last only until the plans for a world organization and the other requirements of an enduring peace have been put into operation.

Even in this transitional time of planning it would be the part of wisdom to seek the direct cooperation of such leaders and groups in the enemy countries as are known to be sympathetic to the building of a genuine international order. The victorious nations should also give all aid and comfort to any responsible or democratic governments that may succeed in establishing themselves in the former dictatorships. In this respect the allies of the former world war failed dismally. If they had cooperated wholeheartedly with the Weimar Republic we might have been spared the growing menace of the thirties and the final catastrophe. To build this greater order and this greater law we shall need all the elements of strength that we can muster. The only way to secure the absolutely essential cooperation of our former enemies is to make them feel that they too can play their part in the new order of things, and in so doing to strengthen the influence and assure the success of those who are on our side. We may then be surprised to discover how many they are. In the transitional period we must be utterly hard against those who resist the new peace and thoroughly well-disposed to those who are ready to advance it.

CHAPTER FIVE

THE TERRITORIAL TERMS

I

In this age of world wars a peace settlement is no such simple affair as it was of old. It must deal with a vast number of momentous and complicated issues. It must be as global, to use a term we are growing accustomed to, as the war itself. This fact creates a serious preliminary problem. No matter what advance plans the United Nations may have made for the peace, the working out of the actual settlement must take a considerable length of time. To begin with, it is a question not of a single treaty but of a series of treaties. There are many countries involved, there are many wars all rolled into one. With each country there must be a separate peace. It is even possible that the war itself will end by stages, that in particular the war in the East may continue after the war in the West is over. But apart altogether from such a contingency, the settlement should proceed by steps, and a distinction should be drawn between those measures that must be imposed with immediate decisiveness and those measures that require the constructive efforts, over a number of years, of *all* the countries involved.

On this settlement hangs the future of the world. There are all kinds of conflicting considerations to be weighed. There are many differences of outlook and of interest to be resolved within the circle of the allies. The creation of an international order is a process that will take years to accomplish. But the world cannot remain suspended for years, or even for many months. Hungry millions may perish while the statesmen debate. The fructifying activities of international trade must be restored with the minimum of delay. The chaos and the internal strife, the scheming and the killing, that otherwise will work further ruin in various countries of Europe and Asia, must be ended by prompt decisions. Even the months that intervened between the 1918 armistice and the Treaty of Versailles caused incalculable suffering and loss. Here then is the dilemma. The total peace is an enormous, difficult, and most crucial business that must consume considerable time, but the exhausted and demoralized world, left derelict after the armistice, must be rescued with the minimum of delay.

The only solution is to divide the settlement into successive stages, according to the urgency of the various issues. There seems to be no necessity to lump everything into one treaty. Two stages at least are clearly indicated. The first should be immediate and peremptory, like the terms of an armistice. It should be foreplanned to the last comma, with all the machinery mustered for its implementation. It would simply be dictated to the defeated countries and should be such as to assure the processes of demobilization and of the conversion of war industries to peace production, the disarmament of the enemy peoples, the establishment of adequate controls over them, the evacuation of all territories occupied by them since 1935, the surrender of spoils and durable goods filched from the invaded territories, the appointment of provisional governments in those areas where the retiring enemy has left chaos behind, the resumption of international trade under temporary governmental guarantees, and the provisioning of the famished countries.

While these measures are being carried out the various agencies already set up by the United Nations should as far as feasible be utilized and extended so as to embrace world-wide activities. The lease-lend machinery, for example, could be most advantageously applied to include the countries where the immediate need was most imperative. At the same time the requisite steps should be taken to assure a stable standard of exchange for all important countries and any other guarantees that would help to set going the wheels of industry and commerce.

The United Nations must see to it that the liberated and occupied areas are restored to civic order and economic normality with the least possible delay. In so doing they should exercise the greatest care and closest scrutiny to assure that those entrusted with the interim administration of these areas, *down to the smallest official*, are both capable and trustworthy, devoted to the task of reconstruction, and loyal to the larger ideals of the victorious nations. Consideration of expediency should be rejected and political intrigues firmly suppressed, until the time comes when these areas are released from control and given the liberty to choose their own rulers. The administrations appointed by the United Nations should be selected with the greatest possible consideration for their qualities of initiative and insight, since the tasks they will have to perform call for all the understanding and all the leadership that can be brought to bear. The problems they will have to face, the confusions they will have to unravel, the divisions they will have to compose will tax to the utmost the best abilities we can find. In this regard it is of primary importance that the military authorities over the occupied and protected areas should have a cooperative attitude to the civilian agents and should not, except on grounds of clear military necessity, direct, interfere with, or encroach on the various projects of social and economic reconstruction.

Next in urgency to these measures is the definitive determination of boundaries, with all that is therein implied. But the redrawing of the map should be done in the clear vision of the principles and conditions of enduring peace. For unless this vision, this faith, is brought to the peace table by our leaders they will again be sowing the seeds of future wars.

While these essential activities are in progress the second part of the settlement can be matured. It would be devoted to the whole elaborate business of organizing the world for enduring peace. This second part of the settlement should not be sheerly dictatorial, as the first must be. Representatives of the defeated countries should be heard and their pleas given what weight seems proper. If the official representatives of any of these countries should prove reactionary or uncooperative, steps should be taken to consult instead the more congenial leaders of opinion in the country. To some people this proposal will seem to exhibit an absurd tenderness for the feelings of our enemies, but we are at this stage devoting ourselves to the making of peace, no longer of war; and it may be well to recall that of all the treaties drawn up to liquidate the First World War the only one that stood the test of time was the treaty in the negotiation of which the principle of consultation was applied, the Treaty of Lausanne concluded with Turkey in 1923.

The proposal for a settlement by stages as here advocated should not be confused with the proposal, now favored in certain quarters, that there be a "cooling-off period" before the United Nations conclude a final peace. We regard the latter suggestion as definitely dangerous. No time should be lost, no needless delays interposed. No opportunity should be given to old interests to regain dominance and thus obstruct the building of a better world. The so-called "cooling-off period" would become a period in which ancient evils would gain head, in which ancient feuds would be accentuated and ancient animosities run riot. We are advocating not deliberate delay but determinate speed. What we maintain is that the quickest as well as the surest way to liquidate the war and to establish an international system is to embody these objectives in separate instruments. The first would deal with restitution and rehabilitation. The terms of restitution should be dictated and the machinery for their enforcement should be brought into operation with the utmost promptitude. The task of rehabilitation and the concomitant reconstruction of an international economy should be undertaken and accomplished as quickly and as thoroughly as possible. At the same time, the project of an international order together with its principles and main features should be proclaimed by the United Nations, and the general plan for its attainment presented. From the first moment of the peace, or earlier, the augury of the more abiding peace should be given to the world, and the preliminary organization set up, empowered to carry the program into effect. But this program requires the cooperation of all nations. Therefore, at the earliest opportunity, the new governments of the defeated states should be invited to participate with all the rest in the epoch-making construction of an international order —not merely a new order but the very first of its kind.

2

A territorial reapportionment that looks toward the goal of abiding peace will be different in very important respects from one that assumes the likelihood of new world-embracing wars in the calculable future. The policy we are setting forth is squarely based on the assumption that enduring peace is attainable. Consequently it calls for certain acts of foresight, forbearance, and even abnegation that on other premises would be useless, or even foolish. The redrawing of the map must be in harmony with the inclusive program of world organization. The two must be planned together. We must remember that, should a genuine international order once be established, our views on many issues involving national advantage or glory or gain will gradually accommodate themselves. Our traditional views about peace settlements belong to the world of warring states. They must be corrected if our will to abolish war as an institution is firm, if we have the wisdom to care for the future more than for the past, if we evaluate the needs of the future above the inherited passions of the present.

At the peace table the most contentious of all issues will be the demarcation of the new frontiers. It may create serious divisions between the statesmen assembled there; and the final decisions, no matter how wise, will be apt to engender new sources of resentment among peoples already tense with hatreds. More than any other aspect of the settlement this one will be fraught with danger to the constructive proposals of the peace. Nowhere is the ethnocentric shortsightedness of men so likely to prevail over their intelligence and over their own interest.

In the contention over boundaries principles and motivations of different sorts are dubiously combined. We may consider these as falling under three main heads: *restitution, self-determination,* and *aggrandizement.*

The ground of restitution is put forward in the simple name of justice. The claim is obviously cogent where an autonomous people has been invaded and subjected to the oppression of an invader. Scarcely any one will question the claims of Belgium and Holland and France and Denmark and Norway and Yugoslavia and Greece and Poland and Czechoslovakia and China and Thailand to have their national integrity restored to them. It does not follow that in every instance justice requires the resumption of the former boundaries. Certainly no such monstrosity as the "Polish Corridor" should ever reappear on the map. There were other boundaries, such as those of Hungary and of Austria, that have engendered extreme and perfectly understandable resentments. These should certainly be changed. The further question arises in certain cases whether restitution should mean a return to the boundaries of 1939, to those of 1914, or perhaps to an even older disposition. Thus the question might very well be raised whether Lithuania, Latvia, and Estonia should be restored as independent states—a question to which we shall return. From a different point of view we might raise the question whether Korea should not be restored to its old autonomy.

These questions bring us to the second ground, *self-determination*. We know the prominence given to this claim after the First World War, under the leadership of President Wilson. We know that the manner in which it was put into effect had

certain deplorable consequences. Some of the states that
emerged in the process, particularly Finland, Poland, and
Czechoslovakia, had adequate tradition, solidarity and "room"
to exist in their own right as states. In other instances the ground
of self-determination was conveniently invoked in order to
weaken countries whose future power was feared. The dissolu-
tion of Austria-Hungary was carried out with little regard for
the well-being or even, as in the case of Austria, the viability
of the new-born states. The erection of three little Baltic
provinces into states had no mandate from history and no
justification in logic. If the Estonians and the Letts were to be
autonomous peoples, why not the Moravians, the Croatians,
the Ruthenians, or even the Bretons? The full application of
this "principle" would have converted Europe into a crazy
mosaic of a thousand pieces. The transparent motive for this
specious exercise in "self-determination" was the fear of Soviet
Russia and the desire to exclude her from the Baltic. Even where
the claim to self-determination is tenable, it should be admitted
only under a proviso that will avoid the creation of thorny
little sovereignties on a continent that already has too many for
its own comfort. If we must create more tiny states, let it be
only so far as they can be linked with other states into some
kind of federal union.

We turn to the third ground, *aggrandizement,* without question the dominant ground for the redrawing of the map that
has at all times followed warfare. The inclusive motive of
aggrandizement is reinforced by a variety of other motives and
is defended by a variety of arguments. One motive is to hurt
the ex-enemy, whether in the name of reparation for the losses
he has inflicted on the victors or in the name of punishment
for his guilt in causing the war. Another motive is to weaken
his military power, by diminishing his territorial control, de-
priving him of essential resources, and especially by seizing
strategic positions such as stronger and more defensible
frontiers, the banks of a great river, a chain of mountains, an

outlet to the sea, and the various outposts of empire, ports, fortified islands, straits and other avenues of communication. A third motive is to gain an economic advantage over him, through the acquisition of territories rich in raw materials, the seizure of colonies, the control of trade routes and the establishment of "spheres of influence". These blending motives lie back of, or at least cooperate with, the general aim of aggrandizement, the perpetual will of countries to expand their borders, to become bigger and prouder and more powerful. The first two grounds of territorial reapportionment have double force when they serve also the third. The motive of aggrandizement is often masked by arguments resting on the grounds of restitution and even of self-determination.

Here, more than anywhere else, we are faced with sheer alternatives. Which do we want the more? Do we prefer to give rein to national ambitions, to gratify our national egoisms, to exalt our independent sovereignties, to press for vengeance, to clutch at immediate gains even though they prove as abortive and finally disastrous as those for which Clemenceau and Lloyd George and the rest of them fulminated at Versailles? Or do we prefer to build a better, more secure, and happier world from which, so far as our best calculations can go, the overwhelming ruin and suffering of war will, for at least a considerable time to come, be removed?

There is nothing more certain than that the danger of war, in the days of our children, will depend on the manner in which we approach the peace. The alternatives are insistent. If we recognize them, if we realize that we can indulge our group egoisms and our ethnocentric passions only at tremendous price to be exacted from our children, there will be no question of our choice. Hatred and pride and fear and the impulse of vengeance and the lust for spoils are notoriously bad guides, but here they are ominous beyond conception.

It belongs to the profound irony of human relationships that in the pregnant period of peacemaking our blind emotions

and our short-sighted calculations often find their fullest vent.
"Woe to the vanquished" is an ancient slogan. The victors take
vengeance, exact retribution. Sometimes, though rarely, the
cause for which the victors have fought is vastly more righteous
than the cause of the vanquished. Our cause in this war has
that rare distinction, in the sense that the *immediate* responsibility for all its devastation lies on our enemies. But back of
1939 there is Versailles, there are the afflictions of Germany in
the years that followed. The Führer is the deadly offspring
of these sufferings and humiliations. With this judgment the
reader may agree or he may violently disagree. So far as the
issue before us is concerned it makes no difference. For what
is vengeance? Whose is it? What function does it serve? In
the settlement of disputes between man and man we have long
ceased to permit either party to take vengeance on the other.
We have discarded it as barbaric, and as socially destructive.
It is no less barbaric, and it is infinitely more destructive, when
invoked by nation against nation. What is this vengeance?
Where all have passed through terrible sufferings, shall we say
that those who are responsible must suffer yet more in return
for the sufferings of the rest? What reckoning is this? What
sort of insensate and befuddled thinking presumes to calculate
the sum of suffering, and having done so proposes to inflict
more suffering in order to "right the balance"?

If instead we support the main motive of aggrandizement by
adducing the military advantage of holding the enemy's strategic points or truncating his territory we again are making a
very dangerous claim. There may have been times and conditions when a country could increase its protection against war
by gaining new frontiers at the cost of other countries. But
it is quite unlikely that under modern conditions this end can
be thus attained. In the first place the seizure of their land gives
the vanquished the strongest of all incentives to instigate another war. The defeated country at length recovers, musters
new forces and seeks allies. The wounded sense of national

unity and national pride dominates all its policies. No peace can be secure, no international order can be built, so long as this wound rankles. In the second place the transformation of warfare renders anachronistic the traditional ideas of security and protection. The bomber is indifferent to frontiers. Mountains are traversed as easily as plains. The narrow seas cannot keep him back, and even the oceans are ceasing to be barriers. Amphibian forces are being developed that can ride the water as easily as they travel over the land. Fortified frontier lines may be an extravagant waste and a delusion, as the French unhappily found. Surely it is folly to create gross dangers to peace for the sake of such illusory assurances.

Let us look next at the economic argument. We do not deny that the extension of dominion over areas rich in essential resources brings with it, *in the absence of an assured international order,* certain military advantages and increases the power of the country so aggrandized. These advantages may be of primary importance in time of war, and they have a relative economic importance when other countries are denied equal trade access to the resources in question and when generally a policy of trade restrictions prevails. But an international order, as we elsewhere show, requires the abandonment of this policy, and at the same time destroys the only logical basis for it, which is the military one. If the annexed territory is an integral part of the conquered country, with respect to its population and its culture, the warlike expenditures necessary to guard it will certainly far exceed whatever economic profit it may yield. If on the other hand the territory taken from the enemy is his external acquisitions or colonies, the relative economic gain arising from the dominant or exclusive usufruct of the possessor is certainly insignificant compared with the absolute all-round gain deriving from a system giving equal access to all nations while at the same time liberating international trade.

Under such conditions it may well be, as various economists have argued, that the net economic advantage of colonial possessions is nothing or less than nothing. Where international trade is not shackled, as it was in the period prior to the war, small countries can be as prosperous as great ones and countries without colonies as countries owning large portions of the earth. Examples like that of Sweden have shown how prosperous, so long as trade is not blocked by national barriers, a small country can be with practically no colonies at all. Germany herself has demonstrated how strong a great industrial country can become though lacking colonial possessions. Her former colonies would have added little to her strength. But this is a subject into which we must enter more fully at a later stage.

To resume, the whole array of passion-fed arguments for expanded frontiers lose all relevance and worth when set against the opposing argument for enduring peace. Certain changes of frontier are desirable, but on quite other grounds. What these are we shall now consider.

3

Let us start with the world map as it was in 1936, before Hitler initiated his program of conquest and before the Japanese began their last and greatest assault on China. Let us assume that the victory of the United Nations wipes out all the territorial gains acquired by the force and the duplicity of these aggressors, as it has already done with the smaller spoils picked up by Italy along the road. What further territorial revisions are demanded in the name of equity and of abiding peace?

In the first place, those countries and provinces that before this war were subject to alien sovereignty to which the people were definitely opposed should be liberated to set up the governments they desire or to attach themselves to the political unity to which they feel they belong. Here the eminent examples are China and India. Manchukuo and the other Chinese territories operated by puppet governments in the service of Japan should be restored to the Chinese system, at the same time that the pledge to rescind all territorial rights and extraterritorial privileges previously exercised on Chinese soil by alien governments is fully carried out. The problem of India is in one very important respect entirely different. The Indian peoples have never, in historical times, created a unified state or even an enduring empire, and thus India lacks the political tradition that China has maintained over thousands of years. With its religious, racial, and caste divisions India can hardly achieve peaceful unity save on a federal basis. The problem of Indian government is a tangled one, and we shall have to return to it at a later stage. Here it suffices to state that the prevailing feeling throughout India is strongly against the continuation of British over-rule. This being so, the only solution is that Hindus and Mohammedans, the Congress party and the Mahasabha, native states and provinces, upper castes and untouchables, get sufficiently together to agree on a workable system of government. To some extent the British have prepared the way, particularly through the development of the Executive Council, largely manned by Indians. Hence, while the difficulties of effective unity are still very serious, they are not insuperable if the federal principle is skilfully invoked. A self-governing India, on a federal basis, is clearly demanded as part of a world order dedicated to international peace.

In the second place, where any relatively large, territorially compact, and culturally coherent group is joined to a state towards which it feels an active repugnance, while contiguous to another state towards which it feels congenial or akin, it should be united with the latter state. This principle would apply, for example, to various border populations of Czechoslovakia, Rumania, Hungary, and other states of Eastern Europe. Its application should be made independent of the consideration whether these groups were allied to the victors or to the vanquished. The principle is intended to avert the needless perpetuation of dissatisfied minority groups, where geographical conditions permit a reasonable solution. But it should not be made an excuse, as was done at Versailles, for the "gerrymandering" of states, ostensibly in the name of self-determination but actually to reward friends and to punish enemies.

It should be noted here that our first and second principles are not reducible to the over-simple ground of "self-determination", even where that ground is put forward in all honesty, as it certainly was by President Wilson. Experience has clearly shown that the general doctrine of self-determination is much too abstract and out of touch with the realities of socio-economic existence. It has relevance only where large and strongly unified populations, marked off by distinctive frontiers, are subject to alien rule. It cannot be applied to areas where different national groups are intermingled. It should not be applied to populations that thereby would be turned into little self-governing enclaves cut off politically from major economic resources and relationships on which their proper existence depends. It should not be applied to populations, however divided from their present co-citizens by language or by religion or by ethnic derivation, that have no burning sense of frustrated nationality. (We mean by nationality nothing else than the sense of solidarity that demands separate statehood.) There is no law written in the heavens that every ethnic group or subgroup must own a state, with all the attributes of sovereignty. Nor is there any reason why self-determination, where feasible, should not be relative, instead of absolute, limited to local or regional control over local or regional affairs.

In the third place, where any of the greater states suffer, as a result of the Versailles settlement or otherwise, a marked economic or political disadvantage such as could be removed by a moderate "rectification of frontiers", it is good policy, for the sake of enduring peace, to sanction the appropriate change. The separation of East Prussia from Germany by the Polish Corridor was an illustration of the exactly opposite policy. Poland should have good access to the sea, but that end, as we

shall show, can be attained without resort to the kind of political surgery that disgraced the Treaty of Versailles.

Another strong case is presented by Russia, which had its
Baltic provinces turned into three little separate states, an
experiment in "self-determination" dictated by the fear of
Bolshevism. These little states had scarcely any other claim
to independent existence. Take Estonia. It never was a state
before 1919. It belonged to Sweden before it was ceded to
Russia in 1721. There are something over a million Estonians.
They are related to the Finns and speak a language that is a
variety of Finnish. Take Latvia. It was always, prior to 1919,
a district or province of some other state. There are altogether
about a million and a half Latvians or Letts. They should at
best form a unit in some federal system, and certainly their
independent statehood is, outside the feudal age, a sheer
anachronism. Take finally Lithuania. Its boundaries are artificial
and are challenged by neighboring states. The very capital it
lays claim to, Vilna, belongs in Polish territory. Its total population is less than two and a half million. Its independent existence does nothing but add needless problems to the peace of
nations. Estonia and Latvia should be restored to Russia which
badly needs an outlet on the Baltic. Lithuania should become a
province of Poland, with which it was in former days con-
joined. This territory, including the Memel area, would give
Poland in turn an appropriate access to the sea and serve as
compensation for the loss of the war-breeding Polish Corridor.

Finally, where the people of any state by a clear majority
evince the desire to be consolidated or closely bound up,
politically or economically, with some contiguous state they
should be permitted to do so. The case of Austria after the First
World War offers the best illustration. Austria, reduced to a
great capital without corresponding hinterland, was anxious to
enter into *Anschluss* with Germany. The victorious powers
and the League of Nations as their agency prevented her from
so doing. This denial must be set down as one of the worst of

the many short-sighted blunders of that settlement. The inclusion of Austria in a larger Germany not only would have saved Austria from economic ruin but would have changed the balance of forces in Germany in a direction favorable to a peaceful solution of her problems. It is very possible that the change thus brought about would have sufficed to prevent Hitler from becoming dictator. But the victorious powers, led by France, were too obsessed by the policy of keeping Germany weak to reckon the further consequences.

We leave for later consideration the whole question of colonies and imperial possessions. The changes demanded in this respect are so closely predicated on the establishment of a positive international order that they will be more appropriately discussed when we face that major issue.

CHAPTER SIX

THE ECONOMIC TERMS

I

THERE is a school of thought that attributes all wars to economic motives or at any rate to economic factors. The adherents of this school believe that the ancient rape of Helen was the poetic disguise of a struggle for trade or tribute between the Greeks and the Trojans. They hold that the length of Cleopatra's nose had nothing to do with the campaign between Antony and Augustus Caesar. They hold that the war waged in the name of religious liberty by the Dutch against the Spaniards was in reality a conflict for the gold and silver mines of the New World. They hold that the World War precipitated by the Nazis in 1939 was the consequence of economic maladjustments, or else if they are Marxists of the old orthodoxy, that it was the last-ditch fight of capitalism against the triumphant progress of socialism.

Many of us are not satisfied with these explanations. They cannot be demonstrated, for they depend on a pre-accepted theory that is painlessly applied to every case. What makes it so easy to apply is that there is an economic *aspect* to all human activity. The real question is that of the relation of the economic to the other aspects. It is surely a very dogmatic assumption that the economic always determines or at least dominates all other aspects. With this dogma we are not here concerned. We recognize it as dogma and let it be. But it is no dogma to hold that every sort of human struggle raises economic issues, and not least the final conflict of war. Nor is it any dogma to hold that economic conditions played a significant role in the making of the war, have been of immense importance in its prosecution, and are of vital concern for the making of the peace.

Here it should be clearly understood that the economic terms of primary moment for the establishment of peace have nothing to do with the matter of indemnities and reparations. These were unhappily the main concern, in the economic area, of the treaty-makers of Versailles. Every economist knows—and it is high time every statesman learned—that a country must meet its obligations mainly by the export of its goods, that if an international economy is to be maintained it can pay only the equivalent of the surplus of its exports over its imports, that this surplus is necessarily a quite limited amount, and that therefore colossal indemnities are an economy-wrecking device, recoiling on ourselves when it is intended to hit our foes. Any economic obligations to be imposed on the enemy should be limited by capacity to pay. This capacity presumes the effective operation of the enemy economy. What surplus the enemy can export under these conditions, and in what raw materials or finished goods it can be exported without disturbance to the productive economy of the receiving country—these are difficult questions that require careful study by the most able economists. When they are answered it will become clear that the comforting idea of transferring to the enemy any large portion of the monumental cost of modern war is a complete illusion.

There is another no less practical reason why we should not insist on heavy reparations—apart from the immediate and complete restoration and return of the durable spoils the enemy has taken from the ravaged countries. It is that the attempt, even the vain attempt, to exact large payments from the enemy country will have the effect of lowering the already low standard of living of the mass of the population in that country. It is after all the common people who will pay the most. We must never forget the first premise of peace, that we so construct it as to secure its future. Most peace treaties have been very short lived. Many of them have been entirely abortive. Even on the lowest terms, it is the rankest folly to undertake the vast enterprise of building a peace and at the same time to set time bombs beneath it. If we enforce a lower standard of living on enemy peoples we shall thereby be instigating the bitterness of class struggle among them; and this form of struggle, for reasons we shall dwell on presently, is destructive of liberalism and provocative of the spirit of war.

The countries that have suffered devastation through direct enemy action will very naturally demand that the physical destruction wrought by the enemy be made good. There is abstract justice in the claim. It remains abstract because it fails to apprehend the economic realities of war and peace. The major costs of war cannot be *restored* to the sufferers. There is no indemnification for the most terrible of all costs, the costs in human life; but we too easily assume, in the hour of victory, that the material costs, or a large portion of them, can be transferred to the enemy. We do so because we think in monetary terms and during war we get accustomed to fantastic figures. When we think of reparations we should think instead of homes and properties destroyed and of the lumber, steel, stone, machinery, and labor required for their rebuilding. We should ask, what materials, what services, can we get from the enemy, directly and indirectly, for this work of reconstruction. What can we get as a *net* gain, that is, without offsetting losses through the disturbance of the international economy we must build?

When we think in these terms our conclusions will be entirely different. We shall then learn to be content with lesser compensations from the enemy, and these should be applied to the countries that have suffered the most grievously while still carrying the burden of the war. From Germany they will go mainly to Russia, from Japan to China. But whatever is done in this respect should be under the direction of reconstruction boards set up for the devastated areas. The task of reconstruction—not the mere piece-by-piece replacement of ruined properties but the planned creation of something new and better to take the place of the old—is one that will thus be in effect an international cooperative enterprise. And if there is any way of making it cooperative in spirit as well as in form, so much more surely will the new order arise through which alone the material and the spiritual losses of the war can be obliterated.

The economic policy conducive to peace and prosperity is many-sided. There are problems of readjustment, problems of reconstruction, and beyond these the over-ruling problem of the greater economic civilization requisite for enduring peace. Let us first deal with the immediate issues of the transition to a peacetime economy. Our whole productive system has been geared to war. It must again be transformed.

At the outset, let us not forget that even a ruinous war brings some economic advances. Driving necessity teaches some lessons we should still continue to apply when peace comes. We have had to abandon many wasteful practices in office and plant, in trade and in transportation; we have had to introduce more efficient methods that save energy and time and materials. These methods we should endeavor to preserve against the unintelligent inertia of our former ways. We have learned that men or women devote themselves most worthily to the task when they have the incentive to cooperate wholeheartedly. We must be concerned to evoke the cooperation of peace no less than the cooperation of war. We have learned that the worker, no less than the soldier, must have his physical needs properly cared for if he is to give his best, that the better he is the better he works. It is a significant commentary on our industrial order that many workers were better fed during the scarcity of wartime than they ever were in peace; that, for example, the Welsh miner for the first time in his long history had balanced hot meals sent down the shaft to sustain his arduous toil. These and many similar things we should not forget.

The war has made the whole world poorer in important

respects. The greatest cost has been the human cost, the loss of workers in their prime, the loss of the creative energies of a generation wasted and maimed and disoriented by war. Another gross liability is the unbalance of national economies, with stupendous national debts the interest payments on which come from taxes and not from productive investment; with plant and labor organized and equipped on a vast scale for an output that at the end of the war becomes suddenly worse than useless; with shortages of consumption goods on every side; with millions of men who must be restored to the ordinary walks of life.

Against these enormous liabilities there are some assets of a kind. Although the income of the war years will have been consumed and literally blown away, although many sources of fruitful investment will have been lost or stopped, there will still be very large sums in the treasury, dedicated to war but now available for the purposes of peace. Multitudes of citizens will own "savings" in the form of war bonds. While these "savings" do not represent productive goods but are "promises to pay" on the part of governments, they constitute a power of demand that can be released in such a way as to sustain productive enterprises through a transition period. Furthermore, the new applications of science, the advance of techniques, the skill and experience developed in war work, no less than the massed and improved machinery of production, can be converted to the normal uses of industry and the normal needs of men.

But this task demands great care and most skilful planning. The cry will rise vociferously from certain quarters that government completely and immediately divest itself of its wartime controls. Any such sudden decontrol would be incontinent foolishness. Only those who cannot or will not learn from the experience of the previous World War could think of advocating it. Private enterprise, however beneficial in its proper place, is no magician to bring order, by its mere existence, into a thoroughly disordered world. Government alone can create and re-create the broad firmament of order on which private enterprise can operate for the good of all. Private enterprise has no means, no focus, no direction, for the restoration of a dislocated economy. Government alone, whatever its failings, has the power, the interest, and the organization to undertake the inclusive task. Governmental agencies of many kinds have acquired during the war most valuable experience not only on a national but also on an international scale. They have been preparing elaborate schemes for the transition from war to peace. They alone, though now they must be subject to the democratic processes of criticism and discussion, can carry through the processes by which a peacetime economy, whether it be capitalistic or communistic or socio-capitalistic, can be restored.

During war our governments have inevitably assumed enormous responsibilities. Many of these responsibilities cannot end with the war. Our governments have taken millions from their employments, from their careers and from their training for careers. First among these responsibilities is that of restoring men to their jobs and assuring the jobs for the men. Armies cannot be suddenly demobilized. Soldiers cannot be all turned into civilians overnight. Controlled prices and controlled markets cannot be released without due preparation, without safeguards against the effects of the unequal supply and demand forces that the cessation of war will generate. The course of business activity must be carefully watched in order to provide against runaway markets, against disturbing fluctuations in prices and in wages, against large-scale speculative practices. The level of employment must be made an index for the guidance of governmental policy with respect to the rate of demobilization, the appropriation of funds for public works, the reduction of taxes. International trade must be diligently fostered, especially in the early stages when without governmental guarantees private enterprise may be extremely hesitant.

In short, the whole process of transition from war to peace demands the endless vigilance of government. It cannot, it dare not, evade this responsibility, no matter what economic philosophy its leaders may privately cherish. It is committed by its pledge to assure the employment of the millions on millions of soldiers and war workers who have responded to its call. It has promised them more than temporary employment, it has promised them security and freedom from want. To fulfil this pledge it needs all the economic wisdom and all the statesmanship it can summon to its aid. It cannot shift this responsibility by resorting again to cheap nonsense about making the enemy pay for the war, as the British and French governments did in 1919. In drawing up the economic terms of peace the primary consideration, this time, must not be reparation or revenge or "justice"; it must be the future well-being of the people.

We shall presently consider certain definite measures that must be taken for the building of a peacetime economy, more secure, more prosperous and more intelligent than that which emerged from the First World War. There is, however, one preliminary task of so great urgency that it must be attended to before we can set about the larger business of reconstruction.

The war has brought famine and every kind of privation to large portions of the earth. The population of many countries is weakened and wasted and demoralized to a degree scarcely conceivable. To begin with, nearly the whole of Europe is suffering; from Norway to Spain, from Poland to Greece, children are starving and mothers are despairing. Devastation and spoliation have made the lot of the enemy-dominated countries far worse than that of the others, but all are in serious want. The vitality of youth has been consumed. The spring has been taken out of their year, and it can never be restored. The consequences will endure for generations to come. The first task of the peace is a task of salvage. It cannot be too speedy, for the sake not only of the present generation but of those to follow.

We must feed the hungry, and if we are wise enough we shall include the hungry enemy. Let us do it on Christian grounds if we have the courage of our faith—but if not let us do it as probably the most rewarding policy that we could possibly undertake.

When we do it is the first consideration, but *how* we do it is also of great importance. There is already in existence an organization prepared to carry out this function, composed of representatives of the countries most directly concerned, including the United States, Great Britain, Canada, Australia, and Argentina. This body, having immediate access to the necessary information regarding the available stocks of foodstuffs, fodder for animals, agricultural seed, implements, medical supplies and other necessaries, should be empowered to pool these resources, to forestall such competitive bidding for them as would interfere with their apportionment according to the severity of the need, and to arrange for loans or other credit facilities. There is also the special organization for relief and rehabilitation set up by the United States. Since these organizations are conscious of the magnitude of the need and are preparing for action on a large scale we have reason to expect that their services will be available and effective at the earliest opportunity. In carrying out this program the greatest care should be exercised to ensure that relief is adjusted in accordance with the extremity of the need and that adequate controls are established in the various countries to prevent self-seeking and ambitious elements from becoming the disposers of relief and thus acquiring for themselves authority and prestige.

2

A peace settlement is not a blueprint for Utopia. Its business is not to remake the whole world. Even if the preceding war has shattered to bits "this sorry scheme of things entire", the peace has not the potency to build it again in accordance with our dreams. It has become the habit of many speakers and writers to attribute the war to whatever they hold to be the evil thing besetting humanity, to the loss of religion, to "materialism", to a decline of morality, to the capitalistic system, and so forth. In turn they call for a settlement such as will overthrow the evil thing, whether by the conversion of the economico-political system or by another kind of conversion somehow to be brought about in the hearts of men. Having a wrong perspective on the historical conditions of war and peace these advocates offer a vain prescription. It is the business of the peace settlement, not to remake the world but to re-make, or perhaps for the first time to make, an international order.

Therefore our concern at this point is with *international* economics. Countries with quite diverse domestic systems can still participate harmoniously in an international economic order. Otherwise indeed our problem would be insoluble. The position any country adopts in the whole range from laissez-faire to communism must be a matter for itself to decide. Our present world exhibits many degrees and kinds of what we may call socio-capitalism, dependent on the historical condition, the industrial development, and the prevailing attitude of the re-spective countries. Sweden has its own, the United States has its own, Russia has its own. The socio-capitalistic position adopted by each people is itself always changing. *With this position as such the peace settlement has nothing to do*. Its interest lies solely in the conditions of an international economic order making for the stability, the security and the wealth of nations. As we shall immediately show, these conditions are to a remarkable extent independent of the particular economico-political systems upheld by different countries. An international economic system, securely guarded and properly controlled, is a necessary condition of the prosperity of *all* countries, whether they be capitalistic or socialistic or, as most frequently is the case, something in between.

What then are the specifications for such a system? They are fairly obvious, and they have been often proclaimed, among many others by our own international leaders, such as Roosevelt and Willkie. The only problem is how to carry them into effective operation, how to set up and maintain the necessary organization against the resistances and encroachments of the myopic interests that cannot see beyond their own borders and beyond their own short-lived gains. We shall set out the four essential requirements of this international order.

1. *We must make provision for the removal of the major barriers to international trade.* These barriers were tremendously heightened in the profitless years that followed the First World War and especially in the period after the depression of 1929 and the coming to power of Hitler, when even England at length abjured her liberal economic policy. They were both cause and consequence of the international chaos of the times. This international chaos will not end with the war unless, among other things, these barriers—high tariffs, embargoes, quota systems, and all the rest—are pulled down. The most elementary knowledge of economics is sufficient to show that they contribute greatly to the poverty of nations.

Why then are they erected? Who guards these barriers? On the one hand there are the agricultural and manufacturing interests that seek to control the domestic market for their respective products. Each counts the gain to itself and does not count the tax thereby imposed on all the others. The self-defeating character of a high tariff policy is thus hidden from them. The worker thinks he is safeguarding his job and his wage level; the employer thinks he is protecting his market and his price level. The apparent interest of each masks the real interest of all. On the other hand there are the advocates of national self-sufficiency who demand trade barriers on military grounds. Within certain limits their argument is more logical, so long as the danger of war impends. This argument became particularly powerful in some countries in the years before the Second World War. Aided by various other conditions it led to the complete ruin of the international economic system. Were the threat of war removed the other arguments for high barriers would be deprived of much of their strength. They would be more easily seen for what they are.

The economic arguments are mostly sophistications. Within no country, large or small, would any statesman propose a system of tariff walls between the different areas. Every thinking person realizes that such gross interferences with internal trade would diminish the prosperity of the country and of all its parts, though sheltered interests in each part would make relative gains at the expense of all their fellow citizens. The same principle applies, with only minor qualifications, to international barriers. The one important consideration, when reductions of tariffs are in question, is that the previous system of protection has determined the ratio of production of different industries and that the abandonment of it would involve the costs and losses of readjustment to a different ratio. This is not an argument for protection but only for the avoidance of too abrupt downward revisions. The infant industries argument, the unfair competition argument (the claim, that is, that foreign goods be kept out on the ground that the wages and costs of the country of origin are lower than those of the importing country), the whole array of mercantilist arguments based on the notion of the "balance of trade"—these are for the most part specious pleading based on false economics. They have no reference whatever to the broader issue: whether on the whole protection or relatively free trade is more conducive to prosperity.

There is in short only one good ground for protection as a general policy, and that is the military ground. Protection makes for a greater degree of self-sufficiency at a lower economic level. It might be worth the price, heavy as it is, were we condemned to continue living in a world of wars and rumors of wars. But if we are resolutely planning for a peaceful world, if we really believe in it, then we had better set our course towards greater prosperity with peace instead of towards less prosperity with war.

The calculation of war is to do that which will most damage our enemy. The calculation of genuine peace, the well-founded antithesis of war, is to do that which will most advance the well-being of the whole. In war we must isolate our interests completely from those of the enemy. In peace we should unite our interests with those of other peoples, including our former enemies. We lived, before this war, in a kind of half-peace, exhibiting a degree of separation of national interests that belongs to the penumbra of war. On that account our peace has been the less genuine, the less secure. This condition has been particularly evident in the matter of international trade. The London *Times* (December 6, 1940) has summed up the issue very aptly. "No British statesman," it said editorially, "has hitherto had the courage to oppose a policy advocated by British industrialists or British workers on the ground of the injury which it will inflict on the industries of France or Belgium or Germany, or to reject a measure designed to favor British agriculture because it would spell ruin to the Danish farmer. Yet there is little doubt that we shall fail to achieve any effective international order, or any alternative to the horror of recurrent war, until we witness some fundamental change, generally and reciprocally among the nations, in the scale of values."

The wealthiest and most powerful countries—not least the United States, with its succession of trade-confounding tariffs from the "tariff of abominations" of 1828 to the no less abominable Hawley-Smoot tariff of 1930—have in this respect been among the worst offenders against the well-being of all peoples, including their own. The gross social immorality of those special-interest groups that lobby into being some new barrier against trade with other countries and thereby exact a toll from all their fellow-citizens is unfortunately not publicly recognized for what it is. It is hidden from the economically untrained public by a smoke screen of patriotic sophistications. It remains one of the grave threats to the peace we seek to establish. Our economists are for the most part too timid publicly to expose it. Our statesmen are under heavy pressure to yield to it. Now more than ever, when our hopes are set on a better world, we must learn to deal with this insidious danger to our prosperity and our peace.

2. *We must assure to all countries equal access to the natural resources of the world.* The raw materials of modern industry are very unequally distributed over the earth's surface. Some countries, like Italy, are very deficient in basic resources, other than agricultural. Most countries are supplied with some of them but no country is supplied with them all. Even the United States, peculiarly well endowed as it is, is very dependent on other countries for certain materials. The development of modern technology has vastly increased the range of essential raw products, such as rubber, oil, nickel, aluminum, copper, tin, manganese, and zinc. When countries like Germany and Italy raise the cry of the "have nots" against the "haves", they are thinking primarily of such products. The scramble for colonies has been greatly spurred by the desire to get control of the sources of raw materials. Here too military considerations have been dominant. Countries have feared that without exclusive possession they would be cut off in time of war from supplies vital to their needs or to their designs.

In time of peace there is normally an open market for all these supplies. Cannot we then assume that if the reign of peace were assured there would be no need for any special regulations providing equal access to them? The goods are on the counter for all purchasers, whether their country does or does not own the natural resources themselves. Naturally those countries that were belated or unsuccessful in the quest for colonies will feel some envy and resentment towards their more fortunate rivals. Is anything more involved?

The assumption is too simple. In the first place the extreme disparity of possession operates to make powerful but less favored nations disinclined to accept as permanent any settlement that seems to seal their status. Secretly or openly they will continue to cherish the hope that some day, by their military might, they can win a greater portion of the earth's resources. An enduring peace can not be reached so long as there is left an enduring source of discontent. Those of us who are members of the more fortunate nations must make the effort to understand how peoples feel who are differently situated—how we would ourselves feel if we were in their place. The problem can be largely met by a new deal with respect to colonial possessions. After all, these possessions were originally acquired, for the most part, by the use of force, and the countries which hold them have in the last resort no other claim to them than the force they own. They cannot reasonably expect other peoples, which have later risen to power, to welcome an international order that abjures the policy of force while they themselves retain titles to domination that have no better ground. Actually, as we shall show, all countries, including the great colony holders (the English, the French, and the Dutch), would gain by this new deal. But this is a theme that goes beyond the issue of equal access, and we must leave it for later discussion.

The broad principle of equal access makes certain more limited demands. It requires that the country or countries in control of essential raw materials shall not impose, directly or indirectly, any export tax upon them. It requires that the industries engaged in the production of these commodities, such as rubber, aluminum, and nickel, shall not be permitted to raise the price or to limit the output in order to swell the profits of the shareholders beyond a reasonable return on their investment. It further requires that international cartels or holding companies shall not be permitted to assign different countries to their respective constituents as exclusive preserves for the marketing of their products, whether in the raw state or after processing. In recent times we have seen—or rather have failed to see—the establishment of a whole array of private economic sovereignties, operating internationally, controlling such important commodities as fertilizers, oil products, nitrate of soda, drugs and chemicals of many kinds, synthetic rubber, and copper. These economic sovereignties have held world markets in their grasp, controlling demand and limiting supply. Such practices can hardly be prevented by the separate action of different states. To prevent them an international economic commission is called for, acting on behalf of all nations. Each step we advance in the consideration of the conditions of an efficient international economy reveals the more clearly the need for a supervising organization of an international character.

3. *We must provide for the maintenance of relatively stable parities between the monetary units of different countries.* Any abrupt change in the value of a country's currency, whether in the direction of inflation or of deflation, has a thoroughly disorganizing effect on international trade. The mere possibility generates a sense of insecurity that gravely limits the exchange of goods. It is hardly necessary to add that within any country an abrupt change in the value of the monetary unit, especially if that change is due to governmental fiat, greatly disorganizes all business activity. Only the sheerest crisis could possibly justify it, and even under such conditions better ways of dealing with the crisis are likely to be available. There are of course continuous minor changes in the purchasing power of the monetary unit. With these we are not here concerned. What is at issue is the determinate and sudden change that occurs through monetary manipulation of one kind or another. Such changes marked the period of domestic crisis and international chaos between the two world wars.

It would carry us beyond the scope of this work to enter on the technical problem of how a relative parity between exchanges can be achieved and maintained. It may suffice to state here that the problem can be solved, for the benefit of all countries, by cooperative action agreed upon by their respective governments. The machinery of adjustment is available. To set it up is not a very difficult task. We have had during this war much experience in exchange stabilization, though of a more rigid kind. The relation between the British pound and the American dollar and that between the American and the Canadian dollar have been thoroughly controlled. This control was essential during the war. A somewhat different and more flexible control, extended to all the leading exchanges, is highly desirable for the time of peace. If the appropriate decision were taken, the treasuries and the central banks of the countries concerned could carry it out by concerted action and thus give a new basis of economic security to all countries, removing thereby one of the great hazards of international trade. An international bank, with larger functions than those of the Bank for International Settlements, would be an appropriate agency to coordinate the various activities of interadjustment. This bank should be subject to the supervision of the already mentioned International Economic Commission.

4. *We must undam the international flow of capital.* No small part of the relative prosperity enjoyed in the western world during the later nineteenth and the earlier twentieth century was dependent on the flow of capital across national frontiers. There were great abuses associated with it. There were financial scandals, there was here and there gross exploitation. These abuses were due to the weakness or self-interest of governmental controls. In itself the flow of capital was highly beneficial. It enabled the less developed countries to utilize the skills and the inventions of the more developed. It enabled them to employ machine power instead of muscle power, to introduce more efficient if initially more costly methods of production, to undertake enterprises of all kinds that otherwise they could not have undertaken. It helped them to tide over emergencies. It raised the value of labor. It assured to many countries the benefit of advances and discoveries made by a few countries, and it

enabled the few countries to participate in the resources of the many.

After the war the renewed flow of capital will become of urgent importance. Most countries will be prostrate, drained, ruined. An enormous amount of rebuilding and restoring will be necessary. With their financial resources exhausted, they cannot set their labor and their skill to work on these imperative tasks. In the countries overrun by the enemy the livestock is depleted and the most common necessaries of life are missing. Not only unemployment but intensified starvation faces them. The need for immediate loans from the few countries still strong in credit and rich in resources cannot be overestimated.

But private capital will be hesitant, naturally afraid of the hazards of lending abroad after the war, especially after the experience it suffered in the uncontrolled lending that followed the First World War. For a time governmental support as well as control of foreign lending will be absolutely necessary. The few governments in a position to do so, and especially the government of the United States, must come to the rescue. They must give guarantees to lenders and they must themselves establish credits for foreign countries. They must supervise the loans made by private lenders, so as to assure that they are used for the most essential and the most productive purposes.

It should be carefully observed that the four main specifications for the reconstruction of an international economic order are closely interdependent. Thus the last-mentioned becomes unworkable unless it is associated with the first, the removal of trade barriers. The vast lending abroad of the United States in the years 1919-1920 had unhappy results, certainly so far as the lenders were concerned, because, among other things, there ensued increasing restriction of international trade. It requires only a little reflection to discover that the four stipulations work together in the same direction and depend for their efficacy each upon the others.

Together they constitute a mechanism for the liberation of

international economic activities. The mechanism in question is, as we have already pointed out, relatively independent of the economic faiths or goals or policies on which men and nations differ so considerably. Many economic issues remain outside our consideration here, which is the *mechanics* of international trade. For the most part these issues must be met by each country for itself. Each must go its own way to solve the problems of the distribution of wealth, of the relation of economic classes, of social security. But whatever program is pursued it cannot but be aided by, and sometimes it may be entirely dependent upon, the establishment of an international economic system. With the specific programs of economic welfare the peace settlement has nothing directly to do; with the establishment of a working economic system common to all peoples the peace settlement has everything to do.

3

It is discouraging that, in the discussion of large-scale economic policies, scholars, statesmen and men of affairs alike have so often contented themselves with taking one or the other side as between sheer opposing principles. It is *either* this *or* that, laissez-faire or governmental control, capitalism or socialism, individualism or collectivism, competition or monopoly—the choice being often accompanied by awful warnings of the perils of the one and rapt laudations of the blessings of the other. These black and white alternatives scarcely fit with the picture of the real world. They belong more appropriately to a child's picture of the Day of Judgment.

What concerns us most is that the habit of thinking in terms of these opposites, at least when it becomes wide-spread among the people, creates an atmosphere unfavorable to peace. Karl Marx thought that the intensification of class struggle would prepare the way for the abolition not only of economic classes but also of international wars. The events of recent history suggest that he was mistaken. When the people of a country divide into two sheerly opposite camps they may not elect war but they will certainly elect a dictator. Those who espouse one extreme, or behave as though they did, will thereby drive others to the opposite extreme. In the clash between them democracy is destroyed.

The conditions that breed extremist movements are therefore inimical to peace. The conditions that developed in various countries of Europe after the First World War, the insecurity, unemployment, confusion and frustration that men faced, fostered by the terms of the post-war settlement, were inimical to peace. Fascism everywhere has been the offspring of crisis. Extremity breeds rancor and bitterness and intolerance and violence. The political organization of these emotions is fascism. Men turn to fascism, or to its dictatorial opposite, when baffled by crisis. So they turned to fascism in Italy and Germany and Spain. That conversion is fatal to liberty and in the end is fatal to peace.

The peace settlement cannot secure countries against economic and social crises. Much remains that can be done only by each country for itself. This statement applies especially to the control of economic conditions. There is every reason to believe that the more secure and the more prosperous the people of any country, the less is the danger of their dividing into extremist camps. Every advance in social security, every safeguard against economic exploitation, every improvement in the distribution of wealth, mitigates this danger. The genuine business of the statesman and of the economist is not with such questions as: How can private enterprise be saved, or how can socialism be achieved? They are rather of this kind: How can economic opportunity be more widely and more equally distributed? How can unemployment be avoided and at what cost? How can a minimum standard of economic welfare be assured to all? How can the disastrous cycle of economic advance and retreat be mitigated and controlled? How can the remarkable advances of technology be translated into greater general prosperity? These are the questions every country must set itself to answer. Only by the close and disinterested and continuous application of our intelligence to the actual situation under which these problems arise can we hope to avoid the crises that lead to fascism and to violence.

It can hardly be said that mass unemployment and economic exploitation are direct causes of war. The point is that they breed attitudes dangerous to the spirit of peace. It was so, for example, in Germany under Bruening, when growing unemployment and its concomitants led multitudes to support fascist policies and to believe fascist promises. The threat of unemployment creates the most profound and penetrating insecurity of our modern civilization. It gives a haunting pariah sense to millions of workers. The fascist promises security of employment, and it is the only one of his major promises that he is actually able, at least for a time, to fulfil. For war with all its destruction brings about, while it lasts, the practical abolition of unemployment. Even the extensive preparation for war may have this result, as happened after Hitler assumed power in 1933. If the forces of destruction assure work to the workers it would be indeed ironical should we admit our failure to achieve this goal during the enriching processes of peace.

While industrial countries have still a long way to go to solve this and other economic problems it should never be forgotten that the establishment of an international economic order makes the task much less formidable. International trade, adjusting itself freely to the principle of comparative advantage, increases the prosperity of all nations. The international flow of capital, under proper controls, raises throughout the whole world the standards of living and enlarges the fruits of enterprise. The resources of one country sustain another in time of emergency. The vast resources of the earth are utilized more fully and enjoyed to a greater extent by all countries. The result is exactly the opposite of that which occurred during the period of tightening restrictions before the Second World War. Then international barriers swelled the volume of the unemployed, closed the channels of enterprise, accentuated class struggle, and aggravated every domestic problem.

Given a freely working system of international exchange the prospect that the internal conditions of the industrialized countries will improve sufficiently to prevent the acute development of extremist movements is now promising. All these countries have been building systems of social security. The establishment of an international economic order will enable them to proceed with the task. Scientific and technological advance is opening up tremendous sources of power and placing in the hands of men opportunities for well-being of inconceivable extent, if only we learn to make due use of them. The character of the peace settlement will determine whether we can approach with reasonable hope the further issues of the present and the new challenges of the future.

CHAPTER SEVEN

THE TWILIGHT OF IMPERIALISM

I

In modern times colonies have been the main territorial spoils of war, and the colonial map has undergone vast transformations since Spain and Portugal first embarked on their overseas adventures. Spain's American empire passed away. The important possessions of Portugal in the East Indies were for the most part taken over by the Dutch. Holland in turn ceded part of her colonial empire, particularly Cape Colony and Ceylon, to Britain. In the eighteenth century Britain emerged as the dominant imperial power, extending her sway over territories far larger than those of ancient Rome. In the later nineteenth century the struggle for colonies again became tense. America was now closed to colonization but Asia and Africa lay open. The British and the French annexed large portions of Africa, the Italians coming third and the Germans a belated fourth. Meanwhile Japan began her career of colonial conquest in the East. At the end of the First World War the colonies of Germany were claimed by the allies, and various other possessions were distributed among them, especially under the form of "mandates". The United States remained aloof from this latest development of empire.

Amid all these changes the political and economic role of colonies was also changing. Spain was unhappily obsessed by the idea that the chief function of her colonies was to supply stores of the precious metals. Her imperial successors regarded their colonies as sources of raw materials and as markets for their manufactures. With the development of the industrial era colonies offered increased opportunities for the profitable investment of capital and for the establishment of trading privileges from which the rest of the world was directly or indirectly shut out. In the later nineteenth century the military aspect of colonization became more prominent. The naval power of Britain was secured by the control of strategic ports, islands, and channels of communication over the seven seas. The military strength of France was increased by the manpower recruited in her colonies. Colonies also helped to assure a supply of the ever-increasing list of materials essential for war.

Changes of another kind were occurring, of high moment for the future of imperialism. Always, from the first, there exists a never wholly settled question of relationship between colony and metropolitan country. The issue tends to become sharper in the course of time. A colony, as we are using the term here, is an area non-adjacent to the confines of the integral state that has taken possession of it, subjecting it to the supreme authority of the home country. On this definition Canada is no longer a colony but India still remains one, and Algeria is a colony even though France prefers to call it by another name. Among colonies so understood there are on the one hand those that are inhabited mainly by emigrants from the home-country, and there are on the other hand those in which the emigrants from that country constitute merely a dominant minority or ruling class. The problem of relationship differs greatly for the two types, but it exists equally for both and it usually admits of no conclusive or secure solution for either type, so long as the colonial status is maintained.

Where the colony is occupied mainly by emigrants from the home country and their descendants, the occupants are practically certain to demand, sooner or later, the full rights of self-government. The political ties between the colony and the home country become more tenuous, and in one way or another the colonial status is finally repudiated. Sometimes it is violently broken, as happened in what is now the United States. Sometimes it is replaced by a looser or freer connection that joins the former colony with the home country in a kind of flexible confederation. In this sense Canada, Australia, New Zealand, and the Union of South Africa belong within the "British Commonwealth of Nations".

When the colony is controlled by a dominant but alien minority, an unsettlement and final repudiation of the colonial status may occur in several ways, depending on the cultural level of the natives and on the relationships formed between them and the immigrant group. In various countries of Central and South America a characteristic fusion of natives and settlers took place, ending in the establishment of new states that may remain culturally allied to the metropolitan country but are politically independent. In the Near East and in the Orient the alien white minority does not fuse with the native population and inevitably tensions arise between rulers and ruled. These tensions are not lessened but instead are nearly always accentuated by the continued processes of alien government and exploitation. Unrest increases. The desire to overthrow the foreign dominion strikes deeper roots. It unifies the subject people and becomes more and more troublesome to the dominant state. The larger the subject population and the higher their cultural level, the more certain is the eventual downfall of the colonial structure, whether through successive concessions leading to self-government or through revolution.

As a consequence of these various processes, accelerated in the modern world by the socio-technological developments that foster mass education and mass movements, the colonial type of empire has passed its heyday and is inevitably on the decline. What has already happened in the Americas is now happening in the Orient and in the Near East. The imperial system has broken in India. It has crumbled in Burma and in Indo-China. It is crumbling in Malaysia. Extra-territorial rights have been repudiated by Thailand and now by China. Arabia and Iran have asserted their independence; Iraq, formally under mandate, claims its own. The action of the United States, freely granting complete self-government to the Philippines, has been quite exceptional, but pressures and compulsions have nearly everywhere been at work to achieve, in the end, the same result. Only in tropical Africa, and in the tropical islands of the various oceans, does the colonial system continue in unabated strength.

The economic advantages of colonial empire diminish, and the question is seriously raised whether they bring any net economic gain to the possessing country. The military advantages are offset by the liabilities and weaknesses created by the disaffection of the subject peoples. Technological advances develop other sources of the war-essential products they contribute. The grandiloquent language of Mussolini concerning his African empire is quickly dated. The emotional symbolism of the conservative Churchill ("jewels in the British Crown") sounds like a reminiscence of the old schoolbook in the ears of many of his countrymen.

If we examine a little more closely the economic role of colonies we shall better understand this change of attitude, as well as the corresponding decline of economic imperialism. In the colonizing days of ancient Greece colonies were plantations overseas (in Asia Minor and in Italy) of cultivators who swarmed off like bees from an overcrowded hive. Colonies have served this function in various degrees for modern countries, particularly for Great Britain and Ireland and more recently for Japan and to a lesser extent for Italy. The colonists remain "under the flag" of the country of emigration and thus extend its prestige and power. But the opportunities for this type of colonial emigration have dwindled, over a great part of the earth, so that it is now of comparative insignificance. There are no longer any open and sparsely settled areas capable of sustaining large new populations. The colonies themselves close, or nearly close, their doors. Only by wresting lands from their present occupants can countries like Japan hope to find colonial opportunities for their excess population, and this is a precarious enterprise of war, vastly different and under modern conditions vastly more costly than the original processes of settlement that occurred in the Americas, in South Africa, in Australia, in New Zealand, and other areas.

The claim made by certain countries, particularly Japan and Italy, that they need and must have new colonial outlets for their overcongested populations raises a variety of complicated issues. The size of population any country can sustain is determined primarily by its exploitable resources on the one hand and by its trading facilities on the other. The economic order we are contemplating is one that would greatly promote international trade and thus enable a larger population to be sustained at a relatively higher standard of living, especially in enterprising industrial countries such as Japan. Low standards of living and high birth rates usually go together, and these conditions, creating the vicious circle from out of which the most clamant demand for colonies proceeds, have characterized both Japan and Italy. All modern countries would soon be suffering from serious overpopulation if they exhibited the birth rates of these two. The governments of these countries nevertheless continue to resist birth control measures, and Mussolini in particular preaches the desirability of larger families. The will for conquest encourages overpopulation in order to make it a stronger excuse for aggression.

Let us now look at a second economic function of colonies, that of providing sheltered markets for the products of the metropolitan country. The colonial powers have adopted widely divergent policies in this respect. France has rather closely guarded the access to her colonial markets, whereas Great Britain and Holland have on the whole followed, until recently, the policy of the open door. It is important to observe that the more stringent restrictions placed by colonial powers on the markets under their control have been stimulated by the general decline of international trade that occurred, for reasons already mentioned, before the Second World War.

When international trade was more active and more healthy such restrictions on colonial trade were generally deemed to be inadvisable. They lead to retaliatory restrictions on the part of the shut-out countries, and it must be remembered that the great exporting peoples depend far more on their trade with foreign countries than on their colonial trade. Without going into the complicated balancing of accounts we can rest content with the statement, as put forward by one of the best authorities on the subject (E. Moresco, in the League of Nations study on *Colonial Questions and Peace*), that "the extent to which metropolitan countries have gained from colonial preference may . . . be regarded as small, though particular instances are to be noted." Furthermore, as the process of decolonization proceeds, the colonial territories more and more insist on the right to determine their trade policies in accordance with their own interests.

Similar considerations are relevant to the role of colonies as fields for the investment of surplus capital. It is not necessary for us here to go into an elaborate economic analysis. The general conclusion is outstandingly clear. *In a world where international trade is unfettered the specific economic gain accruing from the possession of colonies is scarcely significant. In a world where international trade is shackled by all sorts of political barriers the colony-possessing countries have a relative advantage, but the very conditions that give them this advantage are profoundly prejudicial to their general prosperity, especially since nearly all the colony-possessing countries are among the great world traders.*

We need not therefore pause over certain minor economic functions of colonies, such as the opportunities they offer for favorable deals and contracts because of political and social relationships, or again the chances for careers in administrative, educational and other positions opened up to the youth of the possessing country. These advantages affect only a very small number of beneficiaries; and cannot seriously change the balance sheet. In any event they diminish as the demand for self-government grows stronger in colonial areas. At the same time the economic costs of holding and administering these areas increase.

The changes we have been recording must be borne in mind if we are to see aright the problem of colonies in the post-war settlement. In the light of these changes, which assuredly have not yet run their course, we can properly make bolder proposals than would be permissible otherwise. To these proposals we now turn.

2

Two issues of colonial imperialism must be decided after the war. One has reference to the disposition of enemy colonies and also of the mandates set up after the First World War. The other is the broader question of how to meet the dangers to peace that arise within and on account of the whole colonial system as it is at present constituted. What broadly ought to be done about colonies in a world that is committed to a program of abiding peace? Since colonies are the preserves of particular states no effective plan can be carried out unless the leading colonial powers cooperate by respectively undertaking measures that are necessary or desirable. It so happens, however, that of the four greater powers among the allies three—the United States, Russia, and China—are virtually free from vested colonial interests. It may not be too visionary to hope that these could persuade the fourth, Britain, to join with them in setting up an entirely new regime in order to abolish the major evils and enmities that spring from colonial imperialism.

Furthermore, the proposals we are about to set forth have at least this cogency, that they embody and express the major principle to which the United Nations have pledged themselves and for the sake of which they claim to be fighting this war—the principle of human liberation. If this principle has worth for the fettered peoples of Europe it has worth also for all unfree peoples the world over. If colonial peoples also demand the freedom to set up their own governments, then any power that denies them this right, wherever it is practicable, can make only vain and hollow protestations of its faith in democracy. There was enough hypocrisy, as the event showed, in the proclamation of eternal devotion to principles made by the victorious powers during and after the First World War. That hypocrisy yielded the bitterest fruits in the end.

First, then, none of the colonies of Italy and Japan should be regarded as booty to be taken over by the other colonial powers. Colonies that have been autonomous states in the relatively recent past, such as Ethiopia and Korea, should have their autonomy restored. Those that have been integral portions of another country, in particular the Chinese territorities seized by Japan, should obviously be returned to that country. The remaining colonies of the enemy countries, the African possessions of Italy (Libya and Italian Somaliland) and the Japanese possessions in the China Sea and in the Pacific Ocean, should be put under the control of an international commission, with certain guarantees for their present and future well-being we shall presently state.

At the same time all the territories assigned under mandate in terms of the Covenant of the League of Nations should be transferred to the control of the international commission. The mandates system was one of those equivocal compromises between high principle and national self-interest that were so characteristic of the Versailles settlement. The proclaimed principle was beyond reproach. The mandated territories were to be held in trust, on behalf of and for the welfare of the populations. They were, in a sense, wards of the League of Nations. The Permanent Mandates Commission was assigned to guard their interests. The "open door" policy was to be applied to the "A" and "B" mandates. The "A" colonies, including Syria, Lebanon, Palestine, and Iraq, were to be conducted quickly, through treaty negotiations, to independence.

What happened in the case of Iraq exposes the fatal flaw in the mandates system. Iraq was to attain its independence almost immediately, on its admission to the League of Nations. The admission was delayed but finally granted in 1932. It is not without significance that the Permanent Mandates Commission, under the control of the colonial powers, opposed the termination of the mandate, on the ground that it was premature. But more significant is the fact that the "independence" at length achieved was qualified in a vital respect, the retention by the mandatory power of military establishments and military facilities.

The other "A" mandates followed a no less revealing course. Palestine presented peculiar difficulties, because of Arab revolts against the fulfilment of the project set forth in the mandate, the setting up of a "national home" for the Jews. In Syria and Lebanon there were various conflicting interests, and the treaties establishing their autonomy were not ratified by France, the mandatory power. The claim of France that it had to protect minority groups was opposed by strong nationalist movements, leading to serious uprisings among the people. In short, the independence promised under the mandates was nowhere realized. The mandatory powers quite naturally found good reasons to retain their control. Quite naturally they wanted first of all to safeguard their own interests, and they very properly feared that if they withdrew entirely from control some other power would exploit the opportunity. The fatal flaw was in the system itself, and that is why we propose the establishment, for *all* mandated territories, of a genuine international control through an organization that is not dominated by two or three imperialist states.

It would be the assigned task of this organization to administer these colonies, in so far as they were not self-governing; to protect them against economic spoliation and to see that labor conditions were equitable; to develop natural resources in the name of and for the benefit of the native population; to maintain an open-door policy for the trade of all nations; to undertake measures for public health; to promote the development of native organization and unification; and to provide opportunities for native leadership to the point where the colonial status may be finally abolished in favor of autonomy. The international colonial commission would be constituted a part of the greater international structure to be described in due course.

The conditions favorable to an abiding peace would be further strengthened if the great colonial powers could be persuaded to transfer their non-self-governing colonies, or any considerable portion of them, to the same international control. For reasons already given they would suffer no net economic loss by so doing. Their economic investments in these colonial areas would be safeguarded, and the areas themselves would be made more fully participant in the larger economy of the world. Colonial powers would no longer have the excuse that they need armaments of all kinds to protect their remote possessions, and thus the problem of international disarmament would be easier of solution.

The prospect of any considerable transference of such a kind is unfortunately not bright. Here is a psychological price of peace that long-established traditions, backed by the sense of prestige and of power, will stubbornly refuse to meet. Nevertheless it would be well if the United States sponsored a proposal along these lines. It would receive strong support from Russia and China and indeed from the great majority of the countries that constitute the United Nations. The impact of this great body of opinion might have some effect, especially since the greatest colonial powers have been most forward in proclaiming themselves the champions of democracy. They might at least be persuaded to declare that certain of their colonies not previously so designated meet the conditions set up for the old "A" mandates, and agree that these be handed over to the international administration. Among colonies so

classified might well be included Indo-China, the Guianas, and
Burma. We are assuming that the independent status of India
and Egypt will be clarified and assured.

Those who understand that the day of colonial empire has
long passed its meridian will be the more ready to support proposals of this kind. Those who believe that international political organization is possible—not some monistic world-state
but a genuine working system of international controls over
affairs that pertain to the security and prosperity of all men—
will see here one of the immediately practicable modes of attaining it. But in nothing are the conservative die-hards more
obdurate, even when professions of democracy are forever on
their lips, than in resisting the unquenchable demand of peoples
to be free, and to nothing are they more blind than to the
consequences of their resistance. There is an ancient Roman
story, told of their king Tarquin. The famous Sibyl of Cumae,
legendary prophetess who had recorded the future of Rome
in nine books, offered them to the king at a price. He refused,
whereupon she destroyed three of the books and offered the
rest for the same sum as before. Again he refused. Destroying
three more she offered the remaining three for the price originally asked for the nine. At length the king capitulated. Our
imperialists are even less ready to pay the inexorable price that
the forces making for liberation demand. They refuse unto
the end. England could have retained the United States within
her greater confederation had she not insisted on her "rights"
against the modestly reasonable demands of a still loyal people.
She could have held Ireland within her ambit had she not
rejected a simple measure of "home rule". She could have retained India in co-partnership had she been willing to confer
on it, without reservation, dominion status.

The complete solution of the present problem of Indian government only the possessor of the Sibylline books could fore-
tell. We do not take issue with the British government in refusing complete autonomy to India in the hour when the Japanese

were at the gate. The mood of the Indian leaders, generated by long struggles and disappointments, was not propitious for the only kind of truce the British dared to offer. The vast complications of Indian unification under any scheme of full self-government entered into the foreground of the final controversy. How the conflicting claims of race and religion and caste will be reconciled must in the last resort be a problem for the people of India themselves. Great Britain has promised India her autonomy at the end of the war. It seems inevitable that India will take her place among the great states of the East, but the process of achieving integral statehood is beset by real perils. To escape them will take all the statesmanship that India can evoke or can summon to her aid.

This subject, however, lies beyond our scope. We return to the proposal that the colonial powers hand over at least some of their colonies to an international administration. This is important for a reason not yet mentioned. If it were mainly or exclusively the colonies of the defeated powers that came under the control of an international organization, these countries might again, and not unreasonably, cry out on the hypocrisy of the United Nations. What is sauce for the goose is sauce for the gander. If it is a forward step to establish an international authority over Italian or Japanese or German colonies, why deny a like advantage to British or French or Dutch colonies? Only a false self-righteousness will defend the distinction. If we persist with it we shall be doing our best, as was done at and after Versailles, to make the very name of internationalism a stench in the nostrils of the peoples. Thus we defeat our own great cause.

Accordingly we must add the following rider to our proposal. Unless the system of international control over colonial areas is considerably extended by the victorious powers, provision should be made for the return, after ten or fifteen years and on adequate assurance that the conditions of peace are being faithfully carried out, of their pre-war colonies to the defeated countries. A provision of this sort might itself have a wonderful effect in convincing these countries that the new internationalism is not a specious front for the further aggrandizement of the "have" at the expense of the "have-not" nations but is animated by a genuine resolve to build a better, more secure, and more cooperative world.

We venture to make a further proposal in the same direction. We would add a long-term provision. We would fix a date, thirty years or so in the future, when, on the condition that the international program of the settlement has been thoroughly established and has proved thoroughly workable, the vital avenues of world transportation now dominated by particular countries would pass over to the control of the same international authority. A step in this direction was taken as long ago as 1856, when under the Peace of Paris navigation on the Danube was made free to all nations and an International Danube Navigation Commission, which has been very successful in its administration, was given authority over it. There are certain channels and waterways of world trade so strategically situated that the countries controlling them gain thereby a powerful wartime advantage. So long as war remains a reasonable prospect these countries would be foolish to surrender their domination over them. But under conditions of enduring peace the argument for their internationalization is invincible. The claim of individual countries to control them remains a threat and a source of uneasiness to all other countries, a token that the regime of peace is still insecure. Foremost among these world channels are the Straits of Gibraltar, the Suez Canal, the Panama Canal, and the Dardanelles. They all connect not merely countries but continents. The chances and changes of historical possession cannot conceal the fact that they belong, in plain equity, to the world. So we propose, as the climax of the progression to a system of international security, that they be transferred, under the conditions already mentioned, to an authority representing the nations of the world. And since this act of faith, this renunciation of the will to dominate, would be the final act of the long process of settlement after the greatest war in the history of man, the day on which it is consummated might be fitly commemorated thereafter as the festival of pacification.

Many unlooked-for events and momentous changes will doubtless occur before the coming of this day. That is no reason for narrowing our thoughts and our plans to the present hour. The future will not be like our dreams of it, whatever these may be, but what we plan now will nevertheless decisively change the future, and the more wisely we plan the more hopefully can we move into the unknown. If we want abiding peace we must prepare an abiding peace.

CHAPTER EIGHT

THE GREATER CHARTER

I

MEN fight with creeds as well as with guns. And before the fighting begins it is their creeds that raise the banners of war. Men fight for territory, dominion, spoils, it is true, but they must be sustained by their creeds. Warfare is a deadly and devout business. Economic issues, political issues, international issues of all kinds, can be settled in many ways, or can remain unsettled. They lead most surely to war when they enlist our convictions, our prejudices, our traditions, our superstitions, our attitudes towards life—and towards death. In this sense wars spring from the cultural order that lies back of the economico-political order. They spring from the values we cherish and the ways we cherish them.

In the making of peace our creeds play no less a part than in the making of war. An abiding peace requires cultural not less than political or economic preparation. We should in the first place seek to understand the attitudes and beliefs that inspire our foes. We should examine them as dispassionately, as scientifically, as we know how, in order to learn what conditions, circumstances, pressures, tensions, frustrations, opportunities have evoked or nourished them, have sharpened them into the gospel of war. If masses of men, for example, prostrate themselves before some new political "savior", there must be some common cause for this general abasement, some profound shock, some great helplessness or loss of security or whatever it may be. Our enemies are humans like ourselves, and if other peoples cherish creeds that menace us we must, if we are to act intelligently, seek intelligently to discover why. There is no task we seem so little disposed to undertake.

In facing it we must consider how the menace of embattled creed against creed can be met; how, at the same time that we seek to establish economico-political conditions conducive to a world at peace, we can promote such guarantees, safeguards, and opportunities for the diverse faiths of men that these too may live at peace and not be forged into agencies of insensate destruction. Whatever we do to mitigate economic and social inequity will also work to blunt the intolerance and violence of ideologies, but there is here an issue to be attacked frontally at the same time. After this war we must set up a new Magna Charta of human rights, of cultural rights pertaining to peoples, to minorities, to groups of every kind.

Here North America has a peculiar contribution to make—the continent of North America from Mexico to Canada. The conditions under which this continent was settled have evoked the most decisive break with the old traditions that make for war. The United States and Canada in particular are countries in which the irrelevant distinctions between man and man are minimized not only with respect to the determination of their fundamental rights as citizens but also with respect to their chances of attaining individual success, their life chances. There are, it is true, some serious qualifications in practice and even some gross contradictions of the prevailing principle, such as the position of Negroes in the United States. But the principle itself has been set aloft. It has been voiced by the great spokesmen of America—statesmen, philosophers, and poets. It is embodied in the Constitution. In many ways it has proved its vitality. It has rejected the superior civil and social privileges of any religion. It has broken the stratifications of class and it has minimized the distinctions of national origin. It has given a new significance to the words "the people", which in America convey nothing of the opprobrious sense of the words, "the masses". Above all, it has divested political power of all sanctity.

The individual here retains no awe of authority. For him the ruler is his fellow-man and the government is no more than the agent of the community.

The importance of this American tradition is that it most clearly sets the lines for the greater charter of cultural liberation. The import of this charter is that the creative impulses of the spirit of man must not be suppressed or distorted or even directed by the state. In this respect the American tradition presents the most complete antithesis of the Nazi doctrine. All the great countries of our modern civilization have, on their road to greatness, moved also towards the realization of this principle. Some of them have advanced further in some respects than has America, but none of them has so thoroughly divested the state of its association with an elite class, of its mystic sovereignty, of its overawing power, and of its dominance over the cultural life. No one of them has made it so much the creature of the common man. No one of them has gone so far in giving institutional validity to the principle of the equality of men, without distinction of rulers and of subjects.

Let us insist again that this principle is the sheer opposite of that which animates the Nazi reaction. America has detached the cultural life from state control, Nazi Germany has harnessed it, totally subjected it to state policy. All human values have become political. By making them all political, mere instruments of their policy of power and war, the Nazis have destroyed at home, and perverted wherever they have conquered, all the enduring values of human life.

They have harnessed religion, so that it is religion no more but only the convenient myth that exalts their racialism, their lust for power. "Belief and unbelief," said the old absolutist Hobbes, "never follow men's commands." In their blind presumption the Nazis think that power can uphold whatever God it chooses to fashion. But their Gods are infected with their own mortality and will perish with them.

They have harnessed justice, so that it is justice no more.

That is just which promotes their cause. That is moral which supports their interest. Brutality and cruelty are legalized, treachery and infidelity are honored, so long as it serves their cause. Has a man "a positive attitude towards national socialism"—then he is justified in the foulest offenses against his fellowmen. The intrinsic sense of justice is confounded. There is no right but expediency, and justice is again "the interest of the stronger".

They have harnessed truth. Language under their government is merely an instrument of policy. The truth of representation is distorted in a thousand ways. Words are bullets. Maps are "geopolitical" devices to support their cause. Every artifice of imputation is ruthlessly employed. If it works it is justified. No vileness of falsehood is wrong, provided it is plausible enough to win acceptance. "We do not acknowledge truth for the sake of truth or science for the sake of science"—so spoke the Rector of Heidelberg University, once a great home of the free mind. And since the voices that would expose the falsehood are all silenced the range of false persuasion is immensely magnified.

They have harnessed the fine arts, the creative arts. This is not the transvaluation of values, it is the betrayal of all values. The great heritage of human culture has been created by the free man's devotion to intrinsic values. The Greeks awakened the free mind of the thinker and of the artist. The Romans built a system of equity. The moderns have created the unprejudiced realm of pure science, pursuing the truth of nature with disinterested mind. These possessions of mankind the Nazis have corrupted. What they have retained they have perverted into instruments of slavery. Often, to deceive the peoples, they have used the names of justice and truth and even freedom, in the very act of betraying all these values.

The poisoning of the wells of truth is seen at its worst in Germany, though recently Japan has notably emulated the example. Everywhere in the totalitarian countries fear and suppression have stilled the free mind, while servile pens and facile brains have sold to Caesar the integrity of science and of art. The betrayal of the mind has reached a point scarcely conceivable to those who live in free countries. Even the animal world is made to bear testimony to the Swastika! Thus a writer in a German journal of psychology, with that complete divestment of humor that often accompanies intellectual servitude, elaborately explains that "the Nordic chick is better behaved and more efficient in feeding than the Mediterranean chick, and less apt to overeat by suggestion. These differences parallel certain typological differences among humans. The Nordic is an inwardly-integrated type, the Mediterranean is an outwardly-integrated type. The poultry yard confutes the liberal-bolshevik claim that race differences are really cultural differences, because race differences among chicks cannot be accounted for by culture."

All this corruption must end, its roots must be cut, if the world is to be saved from a throwback to barbarism. We need to establish a new charter, in its way as revolutionary as any of the great charters in the history of civilization. We need at the same time to prepare a program of re-education, for the poison of the Nazis has been spread widely over the whole earth, even among the peoples who most heroically have waged warfare against them.

Our program of re-education must be carefully considered and judiciously planned. It is not a simple matter of meeting propaganda by counter-propaganda. Our objective can certainly not be achieved, as we have already pointed out, by our sending professional educators to these countries. Nor is it, in our judgment, a wise idea to adopt the policy of "two-way passage", and encourage selected citizens of foreign birth to return as missionaries to their countries of origin. If we are at all perceptive of the normal reactions of human beings to such methods we should see that they would arouse resentments and create embarrassments that would tend to defeat their purpose.

The business of re-educating peoples is not so simple. What above all we should do is to take advantage of the opportunity offered by the inevitable revulsion from the war regime. This revulsion is extremely powerful everywhere, and profoundly so among defeated peoples. After Versailles the victorious powers did their unwitting best to destroy it by counter-incitements. If instead we use it aright we have the most splendid prospect of winning the peace.

Re-education is not the business of a year or two. In this world of hazards it is the safest of predictions that after the war ends there will not be another great war for, say, fifteen or twenty years, no matter what kind of a peace we contrive. We have therefore ample time for the making of a greater continuous settlement. The minds of men will be everywhere disposed to peace. We must confirm and institutionalize that disposition. Re-education must be more by treatment than by indoctrination, by works more than by words. We shall be re-educating the Germans and the Japanese if we show them, when the fighting is through, that we are concerned for their well-being also, that we regard their well-being as bound up with our own.

In the first place we must show respect for them *as peoples*. We must not seek to humiliate or subject them *as peoples*. In the last inglorious "settlement" the endeavor was made, directly and indirectly, to frustrate, to undermine, even to break down, the national spirit of the vanquished. This policy was the kind of blunder that is worse than a crime, for the most resistant thing on earth, the most vital thing, is the sense of solidarity that a people cherishes. The attempt to crush it merely makes it bitter, wrathful, unrelenting, ruthless. No proposal that would place any of the vital interests of these peoples under foreign direction, such as the proposal that the victors take control over the heavy industries of Germany, should be considered. Unless we respect the sense of nationality in other peoples we cannot hope to establish an international order.

Above all we should realize that in doing injury to the national solidarity of other peoples we are challenging and threatening the spirit of the young. Perhaps nothing matters so much in the post-war settlement as what we do to youth—to the youth of the vanquished as well as to that of the victors. Statesmen are old and may easily fail to consider the effects of their policies on the young. They may fail to recognize that youth takes no responsibility for the older generations, even though it accepts their indoctrinations. It must and will live its own life. It is as young in defeat as in victory. If we cramp it and punish it for what the fathers have done we are sowing dragon's seed, and the harvest will some day terrify us. If we menace its future we are preparing a future menace for our own youth.

By taking thought for these things we shall be doing vastly more for re-education than by any possible propaganda we can marshal. In the distraught condition of the immediate post-war period there will be immense opportunities for the exercise of wise cooperative statesmanship. We can thus greatly strengthen the forces that make for enduring peace. We can in doing so give more influence and prestige to those leaders in enemy and in neutral countries who are devoted to the common cause. In the same way we can the more easily discredit those leaders who are motivated by vindictive and partisan aims. It is important in this connection that our statesmen display great caution in whatever support they give the various "governments in exile" that are planning to return and reinstate themselves as soon as the war is over. Their objectives should be carefully scrutinized before they are given any aid or comfort whatsoever. Any support should be conditional on the explicit acceptance by them of the full peace program of the United Nations and, when the time comes, on adequate assurance that their own peoples would welcome them back to power.

Having prepared the way in the manner indicated we can then afford to go ahead with more direct methods for the re-education of peoples that have been indoctrinated in fascist ideologies or affected by fascist propaganda. We can develop schemes of public education to combat the spirit of intolerance, the excessive ethnocentricity, the various group prejudices and misconceptions that block the road to enduring peace. This process of education, however, should not be a one-sided affair. Let us not give our enemies the benefit of it and withhold it from ourselves. Rather, we should join with other peoples, through the appropriate agencies, in devising a system of genuine social education, addressed to the requirements of the age in which we live. We should seek to extend the horizon of the young, so that, while fostering in them the love of their own country, they nevertheless learn sympathetically of the attainments of other peoples, of their problems and of their needs. They should learn that the march of science and invention towards the revelation of nature, towards the conquest of disease, towards the control of power, towards the replacement of poverty by plenty, and no less the achievements of the human spirit in the quest of beauty and faith and wisdom and the profounder satisfactions of life are the common heritage and the joint adventure of all peoples. They should learn that different peoples have made distinctive contributions to this common heritage, and that the assumption of the inherent superiority of one over all the rest, of the Nordic over the Latin, of the Anglo-Saxon over the Slav, of the Gentile over the Jew, of the Western over the Oriental, of the white over the colored, is childish folly, contrary to the teachings of science, dangerous to the common weal, and unworthy of civilized man. Such education is the precise opposite of Nazi indoctrination, but it is also very far from being fully accepted in our own educational programs, expressed in our own attitudes, or applied in our own practices. We might well begin by revising in this direction our school texts in history and in the social sciences.

Educational preparation along these lines is needed everywhere if the greater charter of the rights and freedoms of groups and nations, presently to be explained, is to be securely established, proclaiming to the world the inauguration of the time of more enduring peace.

2

The decent ordering of international relations presents in exaggerated form—raised to more tragic proportions because of the state's resort to force—a problem everywhere characteristic of modern civilization. Every modern society is a multigroup society. All the forces that created it have made it so. It is never a nearly homogeneous unity like a simple tribe or kin. It is composed of diverse groups with diverse interests and of diverse faiths, drawn from diverse origins into the larger community of citizens. It is divided geographically into regions that exhibit different mores as well as different resources. Everywhere the problem of intergroup relationships arises, between economic groups, between class groups, between ethnic groups, between religious groups. *No matter what the form of government, no matter what the economic system, this is the permanent situation of modern society.* The mobility, the specialization, the range and scale of our civilization render it inevitable.

What matters is how we deal with it. The final alternatives are clear. One is the totalitarian way, which denies men the right to be different, which suppresses all groups that do not conform to a single authoritarian gospel. The other is the democratic way, which not only admits the right of nonconformity but builds up its political order and its social unity on the free interplay of differences.

Democracy has here one great advantage, one signal pledge of permanence, that all other systems lack. Democracy and a multigroup civilization belong together by nature. All other systems must constantly fight a hazardous and in the end a losing fight against the ineradicable tendencies of human beings to divide into groups and schools and parties and sects, each following its own distinctive way, each seeking its own congenial goal, each responding to the expansive impulses within it. The complexity and changefulness of modern society, together with the occasions it offers for the organization of groups of every kind and of every size, support these tendencies and provide them with means and opportunities for expression. Democracy and multigroup society have grown together. Each is a function of the other. The future belongs to them both.

The emergence and differentiation of groups created the challenge to which democracy was the answer. In our Western civilization it was the hiving off from a mother church of various religious groups that broke the cultural exclusiveness of the state. These religious groups were not struggling for democracy. Each was seeking the right of existence and of expansion, but in the course of long and bloody strife it became clear that the only solution was the democratic one. The countries that, like Spain, refused to admit it fell behind in leadership and in power. For freedom was here the mother of invention. When the discovery was finally made—so simple, so inevitable, and yet so hard for men to attain—that people could be equally good citizens of the same state though professing different faiths, the principle of democracy was revealed. The same principle had many other applications. It was the key to the unity and the harmony of the modern state.

This principle, however, must be sustained not merely by a general faith in democracy but also by appropriate attitudes and practices. On this score our democracies have still many lessons to learn. There are those who profess and even extol the democratic way of life while they still exhibit intolerance, pride, prejudice, contempt and all uncharitableness towards groups of different social status or occupation or party affiliation or race or color or any one of divers other distinctions. There are those who win some kind of leadership and notoriety by fomenting these passions and prejudices in their fellows. The spread of these tendencies menaces the vitality, even the survival, of democracy.

This whole issue has been far too little heeded in our democracies. We are not awake to the danger. We do not sufficiently realize how group prejudice is ever at our side, whispering to our vanity or to our greed or to even less estimable emotions that are gratified by the misrepresentation of those who stand outside our little circle. In times of stress or of crisis the whisper becomes more urgent and more potent. At such times in particular there arise the mob-rousing, would-be leaders who beat the tribal drums. The appeal is all too easy. We have not traveled so far from the primitive mentality that fears, suspects, hates difference. We do not reflect that those who preach intolerance are the final enemies of democracy.

The worst of them are those who speak in the name of righteousness. More dangerous than those who are spurred by selfish economic interests are the virtuous little egoists who are possessed by devouring passion to regiment other men, to make the world over after their own image. In earlier times these enemies of mankind often wore the cloak of religion. Now they wear the cloak of patriotism; the days of Calvin and of Torquemada are past; we live under the dreadful sign of Hitler and Himmler. Under that sign, however much they disavow it, march all who stir up prejudice against other groups than their own.

We must become alert to combat that prejudice on many fronts. We should disown those who foster it. We should explore the conditions that breed it. We should repudiate and expose indoctrinations that communicate it from generation to generation. Here is one of the most important projects for education within a democracy.

There is a science of human relationships that needs to be developed. Where prejudice prevails it would train people to see things as they are—as science seeks to do in other fields. It would teach them, in their everyday relations with other persons, to see persons as persons. No small part of the cruelty, oppression, miscalculation, and general mismanagement of human relations is due to the fact that in our dealings with others we do not see them as persons at all, but only as specimens or representatives of some type or other. Our conception of the type is emotionally colored, according to our interest, our status, our relative position, and so forth. We do not, for example, see a Chinaman as a man, but as a sample of a curious phenomenon labeled "Chinese". We react to the sample instead of to the real person.

We all carry around these social images. Every group fashions them for its antithetical group or groups. The employer has a type picture of the worker, and *vice versa*. The socialist has one of the capitalist, and *vice versa*. The gentile sets up his image of the Jew, and the Jew responds in kind. The city man has his image of the "rustic", and the country dweller a no more flattering, though otherwise very different, image of the "city slicker". The Protestant has his image of the Roman Catholic, the Anglican of the non-conformist; everywhere through the whole range of our multigroup society these group images, created by differences of station, origin, interest, and creed, obsess the minds of men.

These distorted forms constantly come between us and the truth. They constantly block our vision of other men and other groups. They present a grave danger to social harmony. It is hardly necessary to add that they play a formidable role in the relations of peoples and states. Internal unity and external peace alike require that through social education we combat their power and their hold over us.

Of all countries the United States can least afford to ignore this source of discord. Here is the most composite of peoples, here the most multigroup of societies. Here the doctrine of the equality of men and of the dignity of the human being has been most triumphantly proclaimed. Here the modes and manners of life—the distinctive American way—are predicated upon this doctrine. Yet it is far from having free way. In one great sector, that of negro-white relations, it has never been accepted.

In other sectors it is grossly violated. In still others, it is endangered. The Fascists, fanatics, Ku-Kluxers, anti-Semites are at work, playing upon the superiority feelings of other groups. Differences of national origin are associated with differences of prestige and of opportunity. Minorities of various kinds are subject to serious economic and social handicaps. Some minorities, such as the Chinese, we have treated with disgraceful disregard of decency, even of honor.

If the greater charter of human liberties is to be effective it must be supported by our everyday practices, by our everyday relations with men of other groups. It must be upheld by our attitudes and our habits. The vain and insidious concept of the superiority of one ethnic group over another, of one religious group over another, of one racial group over another, must yield to social education. The contemptuous dominating spirit that brands other groups as "lesser breeds without the law" must be held in check if our multigroup civilization is to enjoy its appointed and necessary partnership with democracy.

3

The principle of the greater charter has already been pronounced by the leading statesmen of the United Nations. It is embodied in the constitutions of many states. What is needed now is to give it a genuine international form, under which the international order shall support, vindicate, and further institutionalize this primary tenet of the democratic faith. The peace settlement should set up international guarantees to safeguard the cultural integrity of all groups, minority and majority alike, throughout the whole earth.

Let us here state as explicitly as possible the principle itself. It is this. The way a man thinks, the values he cherishes, the goals he seeks, and the God he worships are not a ground for intervention or positive action by the state, save in so far as he advocates violence or incites to it or otherwise seeks to deny to other men the liberty he himself possesses under the laws.

With this proviso all men have the right to cherish and to express their own ideas and to worship their own Gods, without interference by any agency of government, without control by any censorship, and without exposure to any "investigating committee". Furthermore, the practices through which these beliefs and valuations are manifested are no direct concern of the state unless they are also a concern of the ordinary criminal law, drawn up not in order to suppress these beliefs but solely for the secular protection of society, solely in the interest of "peace, order, and good government".

The justification of this rule is deeply founded in the nature of modern society. Its increasing scale, mobility, changefulness, and technical specialization have been accompanied inevitably by some measure of cultural specialization, so that it is constituted of the members of diverse faiths, philosophies, convictions, cults, parties, and schools of thought. These variant members are nevertheless bound together by the inclusive loyalty and service of the enlarged community.

We have begun to learn that human beings are united and sustained by two relatively distinct bonds. One is the specific cultural bond that brings together those who think the same thoughts or cultivate the same tastes or worship the same God. This bond is voluntary, dependent on the free choice of each member. It cannot be otherwise, for no compulsion can make men, simply because they live in the same locality or under the same flag, think alike and feel alike and behave alike. The second bond is obligatory but it also is liberated from any sense of servitude provided the first is not imposed as part of the same obligation. For then the community unites men beyond and beneath their cultural affiliations. The sentiment of nationality transcends their differences. So does their attachment not only to country but also to family, city, region. Thus and thus only, in modern society, can men give themselves freely in devotion and service to the commonwealth.

The form under which this reconciliation and fulfilment are

achieved is democracy. The form that grossly rejects it, thrusting men back to the primitive order, denying their cultural differences and trampling upon their private and group convictions, is totalitarianism. The recognition of the two distinct foci of social unity is, as we have sought to show, the express sign of higher civilization. In this respect, as in others, the Nazi system is wholly and brutally reactionary.

Modern democracy discovered the secret of genuine political unity, as against the treacherous front of unity that force can briefly impose; it discovered that cultural differences can live together under the same law, under the same flag. The principle was first applied specifically to differences of religion, thereby removing a ground of civic strife that otherwise would have eternally divided every modern state. With hesitations and setbacks democracy has been learning to extend the principle to the cultural differences of ethnic and other groups. But it needs to be applied far more widely, far more sincerely. Otherwise certain areas of the world, such as the states of Eastern Europe, will remain eternally disturbed, and vast sufferings will be inflicted in the ever-renewed attempt to establish by coercion and discrimination a political unity that can never thus be attained. The minorities treaties included in the settlement after the First World War were well conceived, and promised a great advance in this regard. But the advance was frustrated by the fatal defects of the settlement as a whole. Under these conditions the guardianship of the treaties by the League of Nations proved utterly ineffective.

It is the essence of the modern situation that the regulation of the economico-political order requires no corresponding regulation of the cultural order. The force-bearing state can effectively control the external arrangements of human life; it cannot, without disastrous consequences, control the creative motions of the human spirit. Fortunately it does not need to attempt the latter, in order to accomplish its essential tasks of establishing and maintaining order, protection, and material

well-being. There must be a unified authority that imposes
taxes, determines currency, maintains a criminal code, monop-
olizes enforcement, lays down the conditions of contracts, and
sets up uniform standards to protect and advance the well-
being of the people under the complex and ever-changeful conditions of modern life. Without this unified authority there
would be endless confusion and clash and exploitation. A man
cannot run his business as he pleases without serious menace
to the businesses of other men and possibly also to the public.
A man cannot subject his workers to a twelve-hour day or pay
them under-subsistence wages without throwing grave costs,
economic and moral, on the whole community. In the name
of justice, for the sake of a decent order, these activities must
be regulated. But a man can worship God as he pleases without affecting the equal right of others to worship Him as they
please. A man can hold one set of opinions without in any way
preventing others from holding a different set. *Wherever different thoughts and different beliefs and different values can
exist side by side within the same community, so that every
man can profess and practice his own without thereby, through
the outward consequences of his practice, preventing other
men from the equal profession and practice of theirs, there is no
need for the state, in the name of justice or of decency or of
order, to intervene.* This is the realm of cultural values, the
realm of all the most precious liberties of man. These are the
liberties that are to be proclaimed in the greater charter, a kind
of international "First Amendment" guaranteeing to all men,
in their minorities and majorities everywhere, the right to
pursue their own values, their own old traditions or their own
new visions, without let or hindrance, without prejudice to
their other interests or pursuits, without civil discrimination
of any sort.

Two practical questions immediately arise. Will the United
Nations assent to the proclamation of such a charter? And if
they do assent will it remain a mere gesture, an idealistic pro-

fession, without the prospect or the means of implementation?

The first question can be answered with some confidence. Of the great powers the United States and Great Britain are already committed, indeed pledged, to the principle. The coming great Oriental power, China, has lived up to it perhaps better than any other country in the history of the world, and its leaders would unquestionably support the charter. The fourth great power among the United Nations, Soviet Russia, has given the principle lip service, has embodied it in the constitution of 1937, has practised it to the extent of rejecting distinctions of nationality and race as a ground for discrimination, while it has fatally lapsed from it with respect to various matters of doctrine and opinion. On the whole, however, it is highly probable that Soviet Russia would give formal assent. Most of the other nations in the allied ranks would vigorously approve, and the rest would follow along.

But here the second question arises. What efficacy would the charter have? What effect on practices that so frequently and often so grievously offend against the principle? No one but the most inexperienced optimist can cherish the belief that the charter will signify the end of all cultural discrimination. It is no argument against a law or a constitutional guarantee that some violations of it are most likely to occur. Our own Bill of Rights has been and is still being disregarded and nullified in certain respects. Nevertheless it is incalculably important as a bulwark of our liberties. Its original ratification struck the historic hour in which the great traditions of the Union were first expressly formulated. So too the solemn proclamation (subscribed to by all the nations) of a charter of cultural liberties may well mark a new historic hour in the record of mankind, as the crucial and enduring affirmation of all the human values that have inspired the fight for freedom through the ages.

At the same time we should not rest content with the mere proclamation of the charter. Now above all is the time when men must strive for an assured and definite international order.

Such an order is not established by the mere enunciation of principles but by operative institutions, endowed with authority and power. We would therefore propose that the principles of the charter be reinforced and safeguarded by an institutional machinery providing for appeals by minority groups against serious violations of their cultural integrity. We shall presently be concerned with the institutional frame-work of an international society. At the apex of the system we place a court of International Equity. To this court we would assign, among other duties, that of hearing, in the last resort, appeals based on the denial of the rights guaranteed by the charter. This final court would itself, unlike some other organs of the international system, have no power of enforcement. But wherever any minority was denied the right enunciated in the charter and had failed to obtain redress through the established authorities of the state to which it belongs, the way would be open for an appeal, without subjecting the minority in question to heavy costs or other sacrifices, to this final court, the function of which would be to declare to the world whether or not the charter had in this instance been violated. The status of the Court of International Equity and its relation to the whole organization of international order would be such, as we shall show later, as to give its pronouncements vast importance. Thus it would mightily help to sustain and to hold aloft the primary liberties of civilized man.

CHAPTER NINE

THE GREATER LAW

I

WE pointed out in Chapter Three the general conditions under which alone a genuine law of nations can be set up and validated. At various times in the history of the modern world tentatives have been made in this direction. But at best they have been partial, indecisive, ineffective, baulked by power interests, and qualified by conflicting purposes. The men of Versailles faced both ways, and their constructive work was compromised and fated from the start. Unless law is armed with authority and sanction it is not law at all. The requirements for international order are inexorable. Foremost among them is what John Locke called "an established known law", with "a power to back and support the sentence". Without this power there is no law, and without this law there is no guarantee of peace.

We can now carry the argument a step further and consider the process through which this primary requirement of international order can be translated into determinate institutions. A *new* structure has to be built, and the ground must be cleared before the new institutions can be erected.

We cannot build the structure of the greater law unless we are prepared to scrap those national institutions that stand in the way, along with the ethnocentric attitudes and traditions that lodge within them. We must, in short, be willing to pay the price. We cannot set up the greater law so long as we retain departments of war, so long as we formulate a "law" of war, so long as we have national armaments, ready to enforce against any other states the designs of the individual state. We cannot enlarge the realm of law so long as we cherish an outmoded myth of exclusive and unlimited sovereignty. Nor can we win the enduring consensus of nations, the common acceptance of and allegiance to the greater law, if we harness it to a settlement that humiliates, frustrates, and penalizes the peoples and, above all, the youth of the nations on which the peace must be imposed.

No great institutional structure can be created simply by the fiat of imposition. The foundations of every enduring institution are set in the hearts and minds of men. The peoples of the earth overwhelmingly desire the reign of peace. Never is the desire more powerful and more urgent than at the end of a great war. And yet such a war leaves behind it the legacy of wars to come. War is a social poison engendering in the disordered system an after-condition that blindly craves, in time, for the very evil that created it. The unexampled ravage of this war, the appalling misery of populations under the heel of a brutal invader, the furious hatreds that will be unleashed by his overthrow, the demoralization, dissension, and social chaos he will leave in his wake, the scramble for power in lands where the processes of government have been destroyed—these immediate conditions of the armistice period, together with the resurgent prejudices and interests and traditions that hitherto have divided nation from nation, constitute a total picture that might well discomfit the easy planner of a better world. It needs heroic statesmanship to stem the passions of the hour for the sake of the inclusive need. Policies directed to this end will win the greatest historical vindication. All others will be branded with the judgment that they betrayed, at the most critical juncture, the faith and the vision that redeem mankind.

Among other things the constructive statesman must clearly realize that international law cannot even exist, as proper law, so long as states, pursuant to their claim of independent sovereignty as against other states, retain national armaments. A criminal code cannot prevail so long as individuals are free to carry weapons and are restrained by no law from using them to gain their ends. A federal union cannot exist so long as the component states possess independent armed forces at their respective commands. Likewise an international union, sufficient to maintain international law, cannot exist unless national armaments are abolished. The issue is not touched by the reduction of armaments. Reduction is purely an economic device. We do not dispute that it has great advantages, but of itself it brings us no nearer to the goal of the greater law. *So long as any state owns for its exclusive purposes a single cruiser or a single battery of heavy guns the establishment of international law is still unattained.*

The reason is fairly obvious. Cruisers, batteries, flying fortresses, and suchlike weapons are designed for military employment. They are not adjuncts of the police force of the country that maintains them, to provide civil protection or even to quell civil riots within it. They stand ready for war. They are "the last argument of kings". So long as they are owned by sovereign states they deny the supremacy of law within the area of their potential use. They say in effect: the peace will hold so long as we do not intervene, and no longer. It is the fundamental condition of law that in the area wherein it applies, all established force is unified and available solely for the enforcement of the peace. The established force that operates within the state is unified to maintain the peace of the state, and if and when there is a law of nations the established force relative to the peace of nations must be in like manner unified. Cruisers and panzer regiments are agencies of war. If under a system of international law they exist at all, no matter how reduced in numbers, it can be only in so far as they are converted to a different function under a unified international authority, in so far, that is, as they are deemed necessary for the police function—the maintenance of world peace.

The essential and ineradicable difference between the military function and the police function is that the former operates beyond the realm of law and the latter only within it. It is true that the people of most countries most of the time regard their own military forces as designed to protect them against aggression and to preserve their peace. It is true that in an armed world the country possessing a powerful military force feels, if often erroneously, that thereby its peace is rendered more secure. But these attitudes do not affect the essential distinction. The police force acts as the instrument of law, the military force where no law holds.

We can now see clearly why all previous attempts to establish the greater law have been abortive. The simulacrum of international law that they set up depended on the pleasure of armed and sovereign states. There was no international authority—no international legislature, no international executive and in the proper sense no international court. We are far from denying the historical importance of these attempts or the vision of the men who undertook them. They projected the image of institutions yet unborn. The world was not yet prepared to give them birth. Even when a vast majority of the nations signed a treaty, as they did in 1928-29, renouncing war "as an instrument of national policy", they did so without any intention of inaugurating the positive institution apart from which their solemn declarations were of no effect. They renounced war but they did not renounce departments of war. They renounced war without renouncing armaments. They renounced war without accepting the greater law.

Such declarations, no matter how sincere and how high the aims of their promoters, are no foundation for an abiding peace. If they lull us into a false sense of security they add another peril to our actual insecurity.

The alternatives stand: state-controlled armaments *or* an international police, independent states *or* an international order. There is no middle position. Any plans for the governance of the post-war world must reckon with these alternatives. Unless they make the greater law their final objective, meeting the inexorable demands of a legally regulated society, they will promise peace in vain. The causes of quarrel are inherent in all groups, are eternal. If the groups are armed and not subject to a common law, the inevitable result, sooner or later, is war. States are dynamic organizations. The position of one relative to another is forever changing. Now, as always, new powers are arising, formidable among them the powers of the Orient. These changes can, as we shall show later, fulfil themselves under the reign of the greater law, as do the changes in all other organizations; but if the law does not exist they will surely express themselves in ever more devastating wars.

We cannot expect that immediately after this war, amid all the confusion and uncertainty, the victorious powers will decree an immediate abolition of armaments. They will doubtless require, as in 1918, that the defeated countries be completely disarmed. In the years after Versailles various disarmament conferences were held, with the professed objective of reducing armaments "to the lowest point consistent with safety". As might have been expected, no lasting results were achieved. *The only hope is in a policy of graduated reduction leading by specific and dated decrements to a minimum so adjusted that it can in due course be converted into an international police force.*

This program would contemplate unit contributions from the various states in accordance with their resources and their size. There is no purely logical method of determining these ratios, and in any event a rough rule-of-thumb, arrived at through negotiation and conference, is alone practical. Thus the greater states, including the United States, Great Britain, Russia, China, Japan, Germany, and France, might each be assigned one unit of the world force, with Spain, Italy, Turkey, Poland, India having one half-unit each, while the smaller states contribute severally a fraction of a unit or are combined into groups contributing one unit per group.

One ingenious author, Ely Culbertson, has worked out an

elaborate quota scheme on a percentage basis, dividing at the same time the world police force into a mobile corps recruited from the smaller nations and national contingents maintained within the larger ones. If international institutions could be determined solely by abstract computation of maximum efficiency and counterpoise of forces, this might be a very admirable plan. But many other considerations intervene. The most likely basis for any international agreement is one that will achieve its objective with the easiest transition from our present political traditions, while at the same time providing a sufficiently simple formula to avoid "the nicely calculated less and more" that is so apt to arouse jealousies and dissensions. The concept of a mobile corps supplied by the smaller states is novel and at first attractive. But do we need this kind of separate police force, given a genuine international system? Might it not create new difficulties, even new dangers? There might well be danger in the existence of a mobile armed force of very heterogeneous origins, detached from civil life and from national loyalties, more especially if over long periods it should not be called upon for any kind of active service. The danger might perhaps in part be avoided if the proposed mobile corps, stationed at ocean islands, were designed to function as a kind of international Red Cross Brigade, trained to bring swift aid wherever disaster befell—anywhere on the face of the earth—through hurricane, earthquake, flood, pestilence, or other cause. But the whole proposal lies outside our present perspective.

The reduction of armaments to the assigned minimum should be accomplished over a relatively short period, say fifteen or at most twenty years. By the end of that period the foundations of the greater law would be laid and the various institutions of the international system would be fully operative. A great international celebration might mark the day on which the governments of all states would dedicate and transfer their remaining armaments to the international authority. The armed forces would take the oath of allegiance to the international authority, on the understanding that they would never be called upon for active service against the government of their own country, that they would be at its disposal for any peacetime emergencies, but that, should any menace to the world's peace be created by any other power, they would be wholly and solely at the command of the international authority. From that date their training would be directed, under supervision of the international authority, to fit them for such service.

A force so organized, so trained, and so commissioned would be as effective a protection against the threat of war and warlike aggression as it is possible to obtain. It would guarantee that the law was in the last resort backed by the power to enforce it. In the constant flux of human affairs it is not possible to foresee or to provide far ahead for every contingency. We should above all realize that while law cannot hold unless it can bring its sanctions to bear against the transgressor no law can endure if it depends mainly on such sanctions. It is the general belief in and readiness to accept the law that sustains it in every society. These attitudes are developed within the framework of congenial institutions. The working institutions of the international order would strongly confirm the desire of the great masses of men to be liberated from the outrage of war. The new generations, educated to the new institutions, would gain a new outlook, a new belief in the international society. They would not lose thereby their national loyalties, but these would be tempered to new aspirations and new goals.

Experience would probably show that the international armed force could be reduced to a still lower minimum. The police within a regularly constituted society, especially within any society enjoying free institutions, needs to make very little show of force. It may not be too extremely optimistic to hope that the time might come when the constitutional law of the international society would need not much more support by arms than the constitutional law of the ordinary state. For the latter has, among all the laws governing the political relations of men, the proud pre-eminence that it is maintained entirely by other sanctions than direct enforcement. The nearer it approached this goal, the more securely enthroned would be the greater law.

2

The international code we are contemplating will contain no chapter on the "law" of war. If war occurs after the law is in being it will constitute, like civil war, a temporary collapse of the whole established scheme of things. A "law" of war will be as alien to the code of international law as a "law" of revolution is alien to the civil code. With this understanding clearly before us we can now consider some institutional prerequisites of the greater law.

In the first place it must be made and sustained by an international organization. It cannot spontaneously grow up, like customary law, or acquire validity through tradition, like common law. These other forms of law can arise only in close-knit communities; this law must be definitely made. A world law requires a world organization. We are not here envisaging a world order of democratic states but—what is an entirely different and much less utopian conception—a democratically organized world order. As we have already pointed out, it would be nothing short of absurd to base any international program on the premise that after this war all states, or even all great states, will turn into democracies. On the other hand it would seem no less absurd to limit an international program exclusively to democratic states—that could be no more than another world-dividing and war-engendering balance of power, as fragile and as unstable as any of its precursors.

What then is intended when we envisage a democratic international order? What will make it democratic? What will keep it democratic? We postulate a democratic international order not simply because we believe in democracy, but because the only alternative is an imperialistic world order; a *pax Romana* imposed on the world by a league of powerful states. Any such scheme, as we have tried to show, is outmoded and impracticable. If so, then the following simple requirements are fundamental.

(1) *The member states of the international law-making association, be they small or great, backward or advanced, enter into it, and remain within it, as equal and equally self-determining units or "persons", with an equal status in the making and amending of the international constitution and in the voting on the laws presented to the international assembly.*

This provision is open to the objection that the principle of equality, as applied to states, is purely factitious, that it has no relation to the realities of size and power, and that consequently it would prove unworkable or intolerable. One of the most ancient accusations against democracy, brought forward by Plato in the *Republic*, was that it gave a false equality to equals and to unequals alike. This charge, it could be said, has far greater cogency when we consider the disparities between states instead of the disparities between men. What possible justification can there be for a system that gives equal voting power to Russia and to Albania, to the United States and to Luxembourg —if Luxembourg still exists as a state? The objection is very plausible, though in meeting it we might begin by reminding ourselves that under the present "system" these so utterly disparate states enjoy a still more anomalous equality—that of equal and absolute sovereignty in their relations to one another. But in actuality the voting parity of the small or the backward states with the large or the advanced states, while it gave the necessary assurance to the former, would not seriously prejudice the greater power and prestige of the latter. This conclusion has two grounds. In the first place the executive and administrative controls, presently to be considered, would for obvious reasons fall predominantly into the hands of the greater states. In the second place the power of resources, of creative function, and

of technological development would still exercise its sway—
no longer as sheer coercion but as expressed in economic advantage, cultural dominance, the whole range of social forces
that radiate from the foci of civilization. For these reasons the
disparity of intrinsic power, as against the equality of voting
power, need create considerably less difficulty than arises, for
example, from the same phenomenon as it operates within the
Senate of the United States. Equality of status in the Assembly
of the Nations avoids an endless array of invidious organiza-
tional problems. The simple principle of equality is the sole
practicable one.

(2) *The member states, without reference to the forms of
government to which they may severally adhere, accept the
democratic procedure as applying to the business of the international assembly composed of their representatives.*

The business of the international assembly is to enact laws
on matters that concern the common interest of states or peoples
or on issues that involve the inter-relations of states. Any issue
that is wholly or dominantly intranational shall lie outside its
competence, and the constitution of the international order
shall determine as specifically as possible the limits of its competence. Some safeguard may be deemed necessary by the con-
stituent states against amendment of the international constitution by a mere majority vote. With this exception it is
desirable that the vote of the majority suffice to ratify the en-
actments of the international assembly. But it may be necessary,
on account of the doubts or fears of the acceding states, to
stipulate that a three-fifths majority shall be required.

It is impossible to foresee the far-reaching consequences, the
tremendous impact on all the changes and chances of human
affairs, that would ensue from the setting up of a genuine international order. It is hardly overbold to assert that this institutional advance, with the economic and cultural readjustments
that would accompany it, would inaugurate a new Great Age
of human society. Mankind would be no freer than before

from incessant problems and challenges; but these would be countered on a new level, and the men of the new civilization would look back on ours as we look back on any past of the earth that to us seems barbarous or even savage.

What matters most is that potentialities of human living, now latent, now suppressed by the anachronistic limitation of law within the frontiers of separate states, would be liberated. The recognition of international community would grow interactively with the development of international law. Guarding the law there must be consensus and sanction. Given the consensus and the appropriate organization the veritable law of nations would at length be born. The particular institutional form is secondary—so long as there is some kind of organization accepted for the purpose. But without such organization the tense sovereignty of every separate state will continue to defy the principle of law and order, and will preclude anything better than the maimed and halting substitute for international law that has hitherto vainly claimed the title.

In the chapter that follows we endeavor to set forth an institutional structure for an international order. It is obvious that any such project is not intended as a forecast of the institutional lines that will actually be followed, should our leaders have both the vision and the resolution to grapple with our need; nor is it even meant to convey the suggestion that the international structure should take the precise form we propose. Those to whom may fall the grand task of building the first international system represent so many diversities of experience, interest, and approach that the structure finally resulting from the give-and-take of their joint deliberations can hardly be pictured in advance, even by themselves. What matters most is that they get together with the clear consciousness of their historic mission. The rest can be left to history itself.

A few architectonic considerations are, however, essential. Foremost we place this: that something beyond law, beyond the furthest reach of established law, must be provided if we dare to hope that the tides of change, moving through nations and their states, will not shatter the world order, breaking again in the disruption of global war. We have advocated the greater charter and the greater law. We have claimed that the greater charter is the necessary guardian of essential liberties and the greater law the guardian of essential order. But we have not yet faced the full challenge of our problem. We have not yet come to terms with the dynamics of change. We must not assume that the forms of newly established law will suffice.

War, like revolution, has often been the violent vent of the pent-up forces of social change. If it is to be abolished these cumulative and in the end irresistible forces must find another outlet, an outlet determined by social intelligence instead of by blind impulse. No imposed or constructed order can bank these forces; no code of established law can of itself be adequate to their demands. The inclusive organization must somehow be made responsive to them, or the firmament of order will crack and finally break apart. The continual shifts in the domain of authority, the instability of ever-changing groups, must be permitted expression. Every group, from the family to the nation, is subject to processes of expansion and of contraction. The international law must not seek to thwart these processes. If we are to have a world system at all it must be flexible, able to cope with a cohort of changes—changes in the equilibrium of population, changes in the production and distribution of wealth, changes in the locus of cultural and social dominance. Here then we propose a final institution, dedicated, on the highest level, to the application of equity.

This institution is also, in a sense, an embodiment of law—but of law as a freely creative principle, not tied to its past, not formulated in a code. In the operation of every legal system there is some scope accorded to equity. And always it has hovered, like an unembodied spirit, over the slow transformations of the code. But here it must have more express recognition, more assured priority.

Let us call this highest institution of the international order the International Equity Commission. We conceive this body as composed of relatively few members, say nine or eleven, representing states and state-groups. There might, for example, be one member for the Latin-American states, according to some plan agreed upon between them, and one member for the United States. There might be one member for Great Britain and the Dominions (apart from India) and one member for the Central European states. And so forth. We return to the question of organization in the next chapter. What concerns us now is to show the nature and function of this apical organ of the international structure.

The law is often accused of responding tardily to social change. It becomes the bulwark of the *status quo* and is lagging in its recognition and registration of new needs and new relationships. Any such inflexibility and formalism would be a peculiar peril to the endurance of an international order. Every order must learn to adapt itself to the incessant new demands upon it. But the world order, for generations to come, will not tolerate any heavy strains at the critical jointings where state sovereignties meet. Consequently the primary function of the Equity Commission is to sense the impact of change on the established order and to make proposals for the readjustment of that order in the light of the changing relations of its component parts, basing these proposals on grounds of equitable consideration, fair dealing, urgency, or indeed necessity. The problems to which it will particularly devote itself are precisely those that cannot be resolved by the normal operation of the machinery of law.

It should be observed that our International Equity Commission is not a kind of World Supreme Court. Our conception is different in two important respects. In the first place the Commission would not be limited to hearing "cases" submitted to it from lower tribunals. It has the initiative of making proposals, and the exercise of this initiative would be its prior responsibility. In the second place its main function is not that of interpreting and safeguarding the established constitution and charter of the international order. This function might be assigned to a separate Court of International Law. Such a court would no doubt be composed of men of high legal experience, whereas the proper qualification for the members of the International Equity Commission would be entirely different. They should be men esteemed for their leadership, social vision, and practical sagacity. The International Equity Commission hands down not opinions but proposals. On these proposals, in so far as they needed full international authorization, the assembly of the nations, presently to be described, would pass. The prestige of the Commission would obviously be of prime importance. It calls for men of the broadest caliber. The appointment to membership should be regarded as the highest honor that can politically be conferred on a human being.

To many people this scheme of a world order, buttressed by the greater law, will seem utopian. Perhaps after all it is a matter of our time scale. Either after this war or else after who knows what centuries of devastating struggle there will be set up some sort of international order with its genuine sanctioned law. When we shall come to terms with the logic of our civilization no man yet knows. The end of this war—if it is the end we are irrevocably pledged to attain—is the only propitious time we can now foresee. To plan for it now, with the boldest fortitude, may well be not a utopian escape but the most practical and realistic job to which men can set their hands and minds.

CHAPTER TEN

FRAMEWORK OF AN INTERNATIONAL ORDER

I

THE First World War shattered the political configuration of Europe; the Second World War has shattered the political configuration of the globe itself—the patterns of empire, the balances of power, the preponderance of West over East, the ineffectual League of Nations, and all the rest. Some new configuration will arise. This much is inevitable. What it will be like depends in large measure on certain decisions that must be taken by the victorious powers. It may be another loose uncemented structure to be shaken down by another world war—to the ruin of those whom it sheltered. It may be another pattern of great opposing alliances, each vainly seeking assured predominance against the challenge of the other. It may be a series of continental or large areal confederations, European, American, Asiatic, each setting up a "new order" within its own frontiers. Or it may be a genuine international structure, built on no past model. Since so much has been shaken down there is the less need to follow older models. When the house is burned to the ground it is possible to build from the ground up.

With all the proclamations, inaugurations, and adumbrations of "new orders" to which we have been exposed in these years of crisis it is well to understand that, so far as international relations are concerned, only one kind of order can be conceived of as new in any fundamental sense. Since the absence of established order has hitherto characterized the relations between states the really new order would be an order confirmed by the greater law. Any other expedient would be merely another variation of the "old order". Alliances, confederations, balances of power, have held the stage in kaleidoscopic variety. If we set up more of them we shall be as far away from an international order as we have ever been. We may dress them up with new titles and new pretensions, they will still contain the fatal defect of all that went before. They will still be power systems forever subject to the challenge of opposing power.

It is indeed surprising that so many writers on post-war issues fail to comprehend this patent truth, that they still devote their ingenuity to some new organization of Europe or some Pan-American union or maybe, if they belong over there, to some "co-prosperity sphere" in the Orient—as though such a program were an answer to the international question. Whatever may be said in favor of such larger confederations on other grounds they are as such utterly irrelevant to the problem of abiding peace. Modern wars are fought not by single states but by great alliances. In waging war they become confederations of states. If it is political confederations that engage in war why should any recasting of the system of political confederations be the key to a world order? The source of the trouble is not the existence of too many separate states. A political rearrangement, consisting of three or four huge Leviathans and these alone, would be no less deadly—possibly would be even more deadly—than the present assortment of a few big and many little Leviathans. If we cherish any hope for or any faith in a world order we must, unless we are still blinkered by some form of ethnocentricity, hold to the principle of a global confederation within which the greater law shall run. Anything less than a universal order is no order at all. Anything short of a universal order is doomed from the start.

It is of course true that, in projecting the framework of an international order, the very conditions of organization make it necessary for us to think not only of separate states but also of state-groups. To carry on various processes of international administration, such as representation on executive and judicial bodies, delegation of authority, formulation of regional and great areal programs within the greater ambit of international organization, and so forth, states must act not only as separate units but also as political blocks, geographically defined. Every inclusive system must envisage appropriate sub-systems, if it is to function effectively. But these sub-systems, in this intance our areal or continental blocks, are not regarded as termini of organization—they are constructed in direct relation to the total organization. They may be differently constructed for different purposes. Instead of being an alternative to inclusive organization they are the necessary articulations of the universal order.

In becoming such they may also serve other ends. The state-groups that would operate within the international system are determined by considerations of common interest and common culture as well as of contiguity. The former considerations would more particularly determine where one sub-system ended and another sub-system began. Since under this project the sub-systems are constituted for purely functional purposes, for the facilitation of the international business of the several members, the creation of these *ad hoc* state-groups would not be prevented by the national jealousies and prestige feelings that resist the establishment of more independent and more exclusive confederations. Yet, once they are constructed, it would seem most likely that the benefits of fuller cooperation, for objectives congenial to each sub-system, would be realized and pursued. We might reasonably, for example, expect that economic reciprocities of various kinds would develop within the state-groups, breaking up for mutual advantage the artificial wall of national economic interests.

The institutional framework, as we picture it, would consist of three main elements coordinated for the direction of international affairs just as similar elements are coordinated within the individual state for the direction of domestic affairs. These would be respectively the Assembly of the Nations, the Executive, and the International Judiciary together with the International Equity Commission. We shall now deal briefly with each. As already pointed out, any too detailed projection of the institutions of a future international order would be merely fanciful, since only the give-and-take of realistic discussion between the greater powers can decide which of the endlessly variant possibilities will ever be actualized.

2

The Assembly of the Nations. The question might be raised whether there is any need for so heterogeneous and cumbersome a body as would be representative of the sixty-or-so states of the world. The Assembly of the League of Nations, while of epochal importance as the first institutional embodiment of a world parliament, proved unwieldy, lacking in initiative, inefficacious. It heralded the future, but had itself no future. It might be compared to the first flying machine invented by man. That machine may have crashed to earth after rising a few hundred feet, but it was the precursor of a new age, with consequences beyond human conception. The precedent was inspiring though the model was sadly defective. The Assembly of the League, like the rest of its institutions, was born under an evil star. It inherited a peace "settlement" that revived old and fomented new antagonisms. It was so organized as to be in effect the mere agency of victorious powers. The United States, for better reasons or worse, refused to join it. It was entirely remote from the peoples. It represented not nations but only governments. It had a structure dedicated to the *status quo*, wholly committed to inertia by the stultifying principle of unanimity. Even its few partial and temporary successes were a triumph of need over obstruction.

The Assembly of the Nations, as we conceive it, would be built on an entirely different plan. In the first place it would be based on a settlement in which the great desire of the peoples for an abiding peace would be genuinely met. In the second place it would be invested with authority, as an integral part of an established order for the control of international relations. In so far as it made laws and regulations these would actually govern the affairs with which it was empowered to deal. It would not pass resolutions, like a debating society. Its business would be of vital importance. No country could afford to abstain from participation in it. Its decisions would make history.

The range of its competence would in the first instance be determined by a constitutional charter incorporated in the terms of peace. Obviously it would take under its charge all those everyday regulations of international traffic that up to now have been arranged by special conferences or conventions of the various states. In addition, proposals for the settlement of international problems and differences, where these suggest or seem to require a general rule applicable to all states, would in various ways come before it for enactment into international law. This of course would in no way preclude individual states from still making special agreements or contracts with one another, provided these did not conflict with the inclusive rules set up for the regulation of international affairs.

The Assembly of the Nations should be so organized that the peoples of the component states are in some direct and active relation to it. This stipulation follows from the larger principle that the inclusive international organization should be an organization of peoples and not merely of governments. It would be highly desirable that, where the general system of government permits it, the representative of a country be decided by popular election from a list of candidates nominated by appropriate organizations. Each representative should have some regular opportunity of reporting publicly, before the legislature of his own country, on his role in the Assembly. It would be helpful if, besides the Assembly meetings held at the headquarters of the international organization, sessions were arranged, perhaps every second year, at one or another of the national capitals. The policy followed in this respect by the committee of the Olympic Games might be applied to this far more momentous organization.

Our object in this sketch of an international system is to convey a broad conception of its nature and its operative reality, not to make a blueprint of its architecture. We therefore merely refer to the fact that the Assembly of the Nations would inevitably undertake various other functions than that of making laws to govern international relations. For example, it would vote the budget of the whole international confederation, apportioning the costs, in accordance with a predetermined formula, to the various states. It would receive reports from the other divisions of the international organization, including the International Executive, taking action on any proposals brought before it by these bodies. It would, on the motion of any of its members, take cognizance of any action of the International Executive, and it should have the power to modify or annul any such action, if in its opinion such action contravened any of the laws it had enacted. It might appoint the members of certain permanent commissions, including the International Economic Commission, of which we have already spoken, the International Labor Commission, following lines now well known, and an International Health Commission. These bodies would have advisory and explorative functions, and they would thus supply the Assembly with the data and formulations requisite for some of its most essential tasks.

This brief outline may suffice to show that our Assembly of the Nations, somewhat in contrast to the Assembly of the League of Nations, would occupy the central position in the whole international structure. By the very nature of its task it would not be engaged, as are the legislatures of individual states, in the endless making of new laws. The laws it would enact might be relatively few but they would be of immense significance. Its legislative sessions might be relatively short, though its committees, boards, and offices would always be active. We place it first in the scheme of things, rather than the International Executive, not because the functions of the latter are less imperative or less vital, but because the Assembly of the Nations assures the democratic validity of the whole structure, offers a guarantee that the Executive will not grow irresponsible or dictatorial, provides the broadest basis for the cooperation of all peoples, and alone invests the regulations governing the international order with the full quality, import, and form of international law.

The International Executive. The main administrative organ of the international system we shall call the International Executive. Obviously this body must consist of a quite limited number of members. Hence it is necessary that, unless we adopt the dubious principle of rotation, all but the very largest states join with others to form territorial units for the purpose of representation on the Executive. We suggest accordingly a cabinet or council of eleven, with one member from each of the following states or state-groups:

The United States

Latin America
(All American states south of U.S.A.)

Great Britain and the Dominions
(Including Canada, New Zealand, Australia, and the Union of South Africa)

Russia

Eastern Europe
(Poland, Czechoslovakia, Greece, Yugoslavia, Hungary, Rumania, Bulgaria, Albania)

Central Europe
(Germany, Austria, Switzerland, Italy)

Western Europe
(France, Belgium, Holland, Spain, Norway, Sweden, Denmark, Finland)

The Islamic States
(Turkey, Palestine, Egypt, Iraq, Iran, and possibly Mohammedan India)

China and Korea

Japan
(Together with Thailand, Indo-China, and other oriental states)

India

Most of the above state-groups have sufficient cultural and economic coherence to warrant our proposal that they act respectively as units for the appointment of a member to the International Executive. The chief difficulty here is that presented by the diversity and multiplicity of European states. Each of three European groups we have suggested has a well-defined center of gravity, the Eastern in the Danubian states, the Central in Germany-Austria, and the Western in the France-Low Countries group. The problem is that of attaching to one group the peripheral states, and there is room for difference of opinion here—unless the states in question themselves settle the issue by their own strongly expressed preference for one group rather than for another.

Let us take the Eastern European group as an example. The states of the Danubian basin, where the great river proceeds from Austria through the lands or along the borders of Czechoslovakia, Hungary, Yugoslavia, Rumania, and Bulgaria, have closely knit economic interests. They have also a common history and in spite of their serious divisions they have considerable cultural affinity. Greece cannot stay isolated, and has already shown its desire for a kind of confederate union with some of the Danubian states. Poland might very properly, because of contiguity, historical background, and economic needs, be associated with them. Similar considerations account for our collocation of states in the Central and in the Western group. But the placing of some states remains very contingent. Thus Denmark might belong to the Central group, Finland to the Eastern, Switzerland to the Western, and Spain, in spite of its territorial position, might have greater affinity with the Central than with the Western group. Finally, we may point out that our inclusion of Palestine in the Islamic group is due solely to its geographical position and offers no argument against the design to establish a Jewish state within that area.

The states forming each group would naturally decide for themselves their manner of electing a member of the Executive. Several methods are possible. However it is done, the elected member would become the official agent not only of his own state but also of all the states belonging to the group.

The International Executive is the one organ of the international system that could be and should be set up *immediately after the war*. It might begin as a nuclear organization consisting of the representatives of the United States, the British Commonwealth of Nations, Russia, China, and Latin America. As soon as orderly conditions were reestablished in Europe and the Near East, the representatives of Eastern Europe, Western Europe, and the Islamic States could be added, in the first instance by specific invitation and nomination on the part of the nuclear organization. As soon as the new status of India was assured, an Indian statesman would join the list. Finally, when the peace terms were in full operation, the Executive should be completed by the accession of the representatives of Central Europe and Japan.

There are two very important reasons why the International Executive should be created and commence to function right after the conclusion of hostilities. The first is that the immediate formation of the nuclear Executive would serve as a pledge of the future order. This controlling group would orient post-war political activities in the right direction. Its very existence would reanimate the hopes and aspirations that are likely to be dimmed in the confusions and relaxations of the first post-war reaction. Its gradual growth into the fullness of its world membership would mark the victorious progress of an ideal. The second reason is that some of the essential functions of an International Executive have to be initiated immediately after the armistice. Thus the program for the graduated reduction of armaments would most properly fall within its control, as well as any issues respecting the pacification of disturbed areas. Moreover, as the several stages of the settlement were completed, it would be at once prepared to take over in turn the various permanent functions that belong to it.

These functions may be summarily set out as follows:

(1) To be responsible for the over-all administration of the affairs of the Confederation of Nations;

(2) To be responsible for the administration of all internationalized areas or possessions of any kind, including channels, routes and means of communication or transportation;

(3) To supervise and control the production of all warlike instruments, in accordance with the terms of settlement, and to take interim action for the purpose of preventing or restraining any infringement or violation of the settlement in this respect, reporting thereupon to the Assembly of the Nations with a recommendation for further action.

(4) To exercise control over the international police force, subject to such general regulations as the Assembly of the Nations may adopt.

(5) To undertake whatever action may be necessary or desirable in order to carry into effect the laws or regulations approved by the Assembly of the Nations.

As for the internal structure of the International Executive, it is obvious that, since its members are appointed on a territorial basis, each representing one great area, the allocation of administrative tasks must be determined by agreement among them, subject to the jurisdiction of a chairman chosen by them. The members of the Executive would not, however, resemble the members of a cabinet; they would not each have separate portfolios or departmental designations. Their specific work would be prepared by committees, according to the nature of the task. For some purposes these committees would no doubt follow territorial lines. There might well be, for example, an Oriental Committee, a Central Committee, and a Western Committee, each composed of the appropriate members. The decisions of the International Executive would be determined, in case of division, by majority vote. But since the issues with which the Executive is concerned are of such far-reaching significance, and since it is eminently desirable that the Confederation of the Nations should run no risks through the arbitrary action of its own highest officials, a stipulation should be included to the effect that where three or more members of the Executive register a formal protest against any majority decision taken by it the issue be referred, *before* action, to the International Equity Commission.

The Constitution of the Confederation should moreover be so drawn up as to make it clear in principle and assured in practice that the Executive is at all points responsible to, and subject to the regulations of, the Assembly of the Nations.

The members of the Executive should be appointed for a fairly long term, say five years, and should be eligible for reappointment. An arrangement might be made whereby the Chairman of the Executive is chosen in succession from each of the great territorial groups, the Western (consisting of the United States, the British Commonwealth, Western Europe, and Latin America), the Central (Russia, Eastern Europe, Central Europe, and the Islamic states), and the Eastern (China, India, and the Japanese group).

The International Judiciary. Since within the projected world system international law, in the true sense, would for the first time have arrived, there would ensue the corresponding development of an international judiciary. The focus of the judicial system would be the International Court. We need not delay to describe the structure of this institution, since the Permanent Court of International Justice, set up at The Hague in 1922, furnishes an effective precedent. As in that instance, the judges might be elected, from a list of candidates nominated by national authorities, by the concurrent votes of the Executive and of the Assembly. The great difference would lie in the status of the Court. Given a reasonable, non-vindictive, and forward-looking peace, all nations, under the terms of settlement, would adhere to the Court. As authoritative interpreter it would apply the law of nations to all cases of every kind in which any state presented a grievance or claimed a breach of international obligation on the part of any other state or states. Its decisions, in so far as they were not modified by statutes subsequently passed by the Assembly, would be integrated into the growing code of international law.

Once the International Court was thoroughly established no state would dare, except under very extraordinary conditions, to reject its ruling or attempt to secede from its jurisdiction. Thus one of the greatest advances in the history of human society, the extension to the whole earth of the reign of law, now in essential respects confined within national boundaries, would be at length achieved.

The Court would give a new impetus towards the codification of international law, as it is authoritatively accepted, developed, interpreted, and applied. There will be great need for the continuation, under new auspices, of the work done in this regard by various conferences formerly set up for the purpose. This task and related issues might be entrusted to a new Institute of International Law.

We have claimed that only under extraordinary conditions

would any state be inclined to defy the authority of the International Court. But in the flux and turmoil of an ever-changing world these extraordinary conditions are sure, sooner or later, to occur. Not only to meet such crucial situations but also to give the greater law at all times the tensile strength and flexibility to meet the strains and stresses of new demands, we resort to the crowning institution of our international order, the International Equity Commission. To it belongs the supreme mission of demonstrating that human reason, ingenuity, and goodwill, under the guidance of the spirit of equity, is capable of solving the problems of the relations of the greater groupings of mankind when otherwise they would erupt into the catastrophic violence of world war.

The International Equity Commission, as we envisage it, would consist of a panel of eleven persons, one for each of the great areal divisions from which are drawn the members of the Executive. Each of these states or state-groups would choose its own Commissioner-in-Equity, and it would be understood that this title was the highest honor it could bestow and that it carried with it special immunities and privileges all over the world. Each appointment might be made for a period of ten years and should not be subject to renewal.

The Commission would itself be neither a court of law nor an administrative organ. It would decide no cases and it would make no regulations. Its sole task would be to explore conditions and to submit proposals. If these proposals were not accepted by the states or state-groups directly concerned they would then go before a regular or a special session of the Assembly of the Nations.

Let us very briefly define the activities that would properly belong to this highest embodiment of the principle of equity. They would certainly include the following:

(1) To make proposals for the settlement of disputes arising between states or state-groups, in so far as such disputes

are not adjudicated by the International Court or otherwise settled by reference to some arbitral authority accepted by the parties to the disputes, and in so far as such disputes, after adjudication or arbitration, remain a source of international disturbance;

(2) To make proposals for the reception into the Assembly of the Nations, as self-governing units, of areas hitherto not self-governing, whether colonies or dependencies of any kind, when the cultural and political development of any such area shall be deemed sufficiently advanced to justify its claim to statehood; and to make consequent proposals for the inclusion of such areas within the great territorial divisions organized for the appointment of members to the International Executive and to the International Equity Commission.

(3) To make proposals respecting the transfer from one great territorial division to another of any state requesting such transfer; and to make proposals respecting the transfer from one state to a contiguous state of any population groups or areas requesting such transfer;

(4) To make proposals for the equitable treatment of the peoples of non-self-governing areas, in so far as any issue arises between such peoples and the governments exercising sovereignty over them;

(5) To make proposals for the protection of the rights of minority groups, in accordance with the constitution and charter of the International Confederation, on appeal from any such groups;

(6) To make proposals for the settlement of any grave problems of any kind arising within the International Confederation.

(7) In general, to make proposals for the advancement of the international order and for the adjustment of that order to changing conditions such as industrial transformations, population movements, developments in the modes and means of communication and transportation, and so forth.

logic of rights opposes it. Self-interest, if not blinded, opposes it. Tradition and pride and ethnocentric sentiment uphold it. Men must then give up something if they abandon this claim. But what, in fact, apart from deluding notions, do they give up? They give up the "right" independently to control their relations with other states, which is, in effect, the right of anarchy. For the smaller states this ungrounded "right" is empty, for the greater ones it is illusory. If they abandon it the ever-recurring occasions of strife, the inevitable rivalries and jealousies that all groups entertain, would no longer threaten to destroy the peace and order of the world. Nations would no longer have the same powerful motivation to regard neighboring nations as hateful foreigners with whom they share no community of interest or of well-being. Nor would they lose in the process their distinctive culture and quality, any more than they lose it now, any more than Wales and Scotland and Brittany and Provence have lost theirs within the much closer unity of a single state.

They would give up some things, but only things no state has a reasonable claim independently to regulate, because they concern others as much as they concern itself. There are, of course, various problems respecting the range of things that are the joint concern of several states or of all states, as contrasted with the things that fall within the proper control of the individual state. There can be no doubt that the mode in which disputes between states are settled is a primary concern of all states, not merely of the parties to the dispute. There can be no doubt that such matters as the freedom of the high seas, the access to essential raw materials, the rules governing the channels of international communication and transportation, the mechanisms for the settlement of international balances, should come within the area of international jurisdiction. On the other hand there can be no doubt that the laws regulating marriage, to take one of a thousand examples, are the exclusive right and responsibility of the unitary state. There can be little doubt that the control of immigration, though it affects the citizens of other states, must on grounds of prior interest remain the prerogative of each nation-state. The making of tariffs is a more debatable prerogative, yet the strength of the intranational interests involved preclude any strong likelihood that it could be subjected to direct international control. Perhaps the best we can hope for is that it would become common practice to determine tariff regulations through international conference, and that the very existence of the International Confederation would bring new influences to bear by way of strengthening the opposition to the excessive and dangerous demands of organized tariff interests.

The points we have just been considering suggest some of the difficulties that lie in wait for the international system. It would be absurd not to admit that there are serious difficulties. If they did not exist the obvious need for an international order would already have created one. It should hardly be necessary to add that every achievement of real moment is made in the face of difficulties, and that these obstacles are not reasons why men should abandon the quest but problems to be solved in the process of attainment.

Among the difficulties to be faced there is one that is purely factitious. The International Confederation cannot be set up without a certain diminution of the heretofore asserted sovereignty of every state. It is held that the constitutions of some states, and particularly that of the United States, present a formidable barrier to any settlement that infringes on the sovereign prerogatives of the state and the allocation of sovereign powers within the system of government. For example, under the Constitution of the United States the treaty-making power is vested in the President with the advice and consent of two-thirds of the Senate. Thus if no more than thirty-three senators—or even fewer, since it is the senators actually present who count—representing possibly a quite small percentage of the population, should refuse to ratify a settlement deemed to diminish their powers, the whole international program would be wrecked. Again, if the Senate claimed that under the Constitution it could not vote away a power entrusted to it, or if the Supreme Court should hand down an opinion affirming this or any similar claim, once more the participation of the United States within an international order would be thwarted, and the order itself would be jeopardized. We shall not here take up the pros and cons of a technical constitutional question. We shall not examine whether the establishment of the kind of international system we have described would require a constitutional amendment. For one thing is absolutely plain and has become even more so in recent years—if the people of the United States are widely agreed that they want an abiding peace, and a settlement that offers good promise of an abiding peace, then no constitutional barrier can be interposed. The constitutional means will be available. The Constitution exists only in the will and purpose of the people. Its continuity is the symbol of their continuity. If new needs arise its vitality lies in its adaptation to them. Here, too, the letter killeth and the spirit maketh alive. And we may recall that the Fathers of the Constitution, who differed greatly on many things, were of one mind that all power must be derived from and rest with the people. To which doctrine we may now add a sentence from Alexander Hamilton, giving it an application quite different from that which he had in mind: "The power which one society bestows upon any man or body of men can never extend beyond its own limits."

CONSTITUTION
of the International Confederation
THE GREATER CHARTER

Executive

**THE INTERNATIONAL
EXECUTIVE**
(Members elected
by great areal
divisions)

Legislative

**THE ASSEMBLY
OF THE NATIONS**
(Members elected by
individual states)

Judiciary

**THE COURT
OF INTERNATIONAL LAW**
(Members elected by
the Executive
and the Assembly)

Office of
Armament Control

International
Economic
Commission

Institute
of
International
Law

Office of
International
Police

International
Labor
Commission

Administration of
Internationalized
Areas

International
Health
Commission

**INTERNATIONAL EQUITY
COMMISSION**

CHAPTER ELEVEN

PROSPECTS OF AN INTERNATIONAL ORDER

I

THE problem of government is never solved. It has to be solved afresh with the changing times. For government is the external organization of human relationships, and wherever men discover new resources or build faster ships or invent power engines or harness electricity or dream new dreams they are thrown into different relationships than before, and thereby the problem of government is changed.

In our own age government has vastly extended the *range* of its controls. This was inevitable, because with the growing complexity of industrial civilization there arose a great new tangle of relationships between men and men, between men and their new instruments of communication, of production, and of power, between changing group and changing group. We cannot have automobiles and radios and airplanes and economic corporations and cartels without giving handsome new tasks to government. This spread of government is the result not of changing theories but of changing conditions, though in turn it has excited new doctrines of government.

But here we must make a distinction. The form and the spirit of government depend on our attitudes, ideas, indoctrinations. *How* certain things are controlled and whether *certain* things are controlled at all depend on what theories of government prevail among us. There is thus a vast difference between different kinds of modern state, and the gulf stretches widest and deepest between the totalitarian and the democratic state.

But all states alike are under the sheer necessity of maintaining order, adjudicating disputes, and regulating the conditions of contractual relationships between men. Therefore all states alike have been led to undertake a great many new functions responsive to new conditions and new needs.

Thus has arisen the problem of the modern state. The advance of technology, with its incessant disturbance of established ways and its precipitation of more complex and more extensive relationships between men and between groups of men, has thrust new tasks upon government and at the same time has given it new powers and new levers of power. The more elaborate our civilization has become the more changeful has it also become. Interdependence has grown with instability, and with new resources have come new insecurities. Government is called on to adjust a thousand issues of the most diverse kinds and to plan ahead against the recurrence of the more serious maladjustments.

This situation has evoked the modern conflict of political ideologies. The older conflict between regulation and laissez-faire has shifted to a new area. No intelligent person believes in laissez-faire in the old sense, not because he is more intelligent than the earlier advocates of this policy but because changed conditions have made its premises no longer plausible. No one who understands anything about the working of a modern economy can hold any longer that competition is able to level out difference, equalize opportunity, make the cost of goods the measure of their price, reduce profits everywhere to the point where they become the awards necessary for the evocation of enterprise, and generally evoke the maximum of service from everyone. No one who knows the habits of the multitudes who work for wages or for salaries can still regard the profit motive as the all-prevailing spur of economic activity. Everyone has become aware of the organized controls that dominate business and finance and make the old concept of "free competition" hopelessly inadequate as an explanation of the price system. Every-

factors constitute their explanation. It was not the issue of capitalism, it was the unleashed spirit of resurgent nationalism, incarnated in a ruthless revengeful leader, that destroyed the peace.

Modern war is so all-embracing and so devastating that it comes very easy to men to conclude that the preceding civilization must have been totally misguided and profoundly wrong. The magnitude of the cause, they reckon, must equal the magnitude of the effect. So there are some who blame a capitalism fallen into rottenness, and there are others who blame a godless and materialistic world, and there are others who find that we had grown morally decadent and regardless of our responsibilities to our fellowmen. Once such a position has been taken it is again easy to find enough evidence to make the claim impressive. But perhaps these Jeremiahs and prophets of doom are reasoning from mistaken premises. This argument is too oblivious of specific causes. Wars have occurred in every age, in better times and in worse. The magnitude of the effect may have little relation to the magnitude of the precipitating factor.

That lack of relationship may indeed be the final indictment of modern war. If a war breaks out between great nations, under modern conditions, it knows no limits. *No matter whether the "cause" be small or great, war forgets the "cause" and engulfs the whole earth.* So long as the rulers of states are in a position to make wars, so long as the world is not organized for peace, wars are liable to occur at any time. It is surely then the part of wisdom to endeavor to change the system of government that institutionalizes war and thus to make its occurrence unlikely, rather than to lay the chief blame on other conditions and institutions, however bad they may appear to our eyes, and leave out of the account the institutional organization for war itself, the political system that makes its outbreak perennially possible until at length it overwhelms us again.

Therefore we do not think it necessary, or even desirable, in a book devoted to the organization of peace, to take under consideration the great socio-economic questions that vex and challenge every modern state. If we merge all our problems into one we are the less likely to solve any of them. The problem of war is, we maintain, in essentials solvable, if we have the courage and the sense to face it. If on the other hand we make its solution depend on the solution of other great problems, themselves protean and ever-shifting and different for every state, we shall end nowhere save in confusion.

It is of course true that economic and other factors, in the absence of an international order, are precipitants of war. As we pointed out in an earlier chapter, the "causes" of war, in this sense, are as numerous as we care to make them. Such causes are any matters of dispute between states, so long as states find no better way of settling their disputes than by going to war. Disputes between states can never be eliminated, any more than disputes between men. Since we have already considered the international machinery for the settlement of such disputes, all that remains for our consideration is the question of further safeguards of international order through such internal organization of states themselves as will strengthen the realm of peace.

There are here two possible sources of danger. One is that individual states will pursue certain policies, in areas lying outside the jurisdiction of the International Confederation, such as will grievously militate against the prosperity of other states, lead to reprisals, and undermine the consensus of nations on which the international order rests. Here an obvious threat lies in tariff policies. With the establishment of the international economic machinery already described it is less likely that states will indulge in extreme "protective" measures and precipitate tariff wars. But tariff interests are well-organized and are insatiate, so that the danger remains. If countries are cut off from their foreign markets they are the more inclined to find markets another way, and the only other way is the resort to force. If then the whole matter of tariffs remains exclusively within the prerogatives of individual states some safeguards against this danger should be devised. It would, for example, be highly desirable that the states of the International Confederation accept a rule to the following effect. When any state feels that its economic prosperity is seriously menaced by new tariff measures of any other state and makes representation on this ground, the matter shall be referred to the International Economic Commission. The Commission shall within six months deliver its report and in the interim the tariff changes shall remain in abeyance. If the report endorses the standpoint of the protesting state or states, the appropriate organ of the International Confederation shall consult with the government of the offending state or states, with a view to facilitating some revision acceptable to all concerned. A rule of this sort would in no way affect the autonomy of the tariff-making state, though it might have a very important influence in checking prejudicial demands for higher tariffs.

The other source of danger is the occurrence of grave civil disorder and irreconcilable division within one or more of the greater states, portending the violence of revolution. Such a condition might not only threaten civil war but also lead to international disruption following the breakaway of the affected state or states from the realm of the greater law. In general there have been in the past three types of internal division so bitter and so deep-cleaving that they have destroyed the internal stability of government. One is economic class struggle, the stimulant of most of the major revolutions in human history. Another is the antagonism of ethnic or racial groups, particularly where a dominant race or nationality suppresses and exploits a minority or otherwise less powerful group. The third is religious intolerance, where different religions exist within the same community and regard one another with abhorrence.

Of these three causes of political instability the last-mentioned has lost much of its former virulence, though in many states it still exists as a disturbing factor. In our present world it is, on the whole, only when religious difference combines with ethnic or racial difference that the unity of the state is formidably imperiled. Under the greater charter of the International Confederation both religious and ethnic or racial minorities are safeguarded, and the Confederation has means at its disposal to give reasonable efficacy to this guarantee of the status of minorities. There remains then the first and the greatest of the potentially disruptive forces, the struggle of economic classes. Here is an issue that requires more particular consideration.

2

We have insisted that it is entirely beyond the competence of the peace treaties to prescribe the internal economic policy of any state, and that writers commit a bad blunder—and statesmen a worse one—when they include with proposals for international settlement any program contemplating the establishment of a particular economic system throughout the world, whether it be capitalism, socialism, national planned economy, or anything else. In the pages that follow we are concerned neither with the intrinsic advantages of any economic system nor with any specific policies that we deem it desirable for the International Confederation to implement, but solely with the prognosis of a potential threat to a once-established international order, such a threat as may arise from the divisive forces of intrastate class struggle.

While this danger cannot be disregarded we nevertheless believe that the very existence of the kind of international system we have been describing will do much to mitigate the violence of class warfare. In the first place it will certainly raise the level of economic prosperity in all countries. The sacrifice of welfare for self-sufficiency will no longer have any appeal. With the restoration and improvement of the international economic mechanism there will certainly be freer trade between nations. We may hope too that the lessons of the period from 1919 to 1939 will not be forgotten and that the interests seeking high tariffs and other impediments to international trade will be checked by a wider public recognition of the evil consequences of such policies.

The increase of prosperity will not bring anything that could be called industrial peace. Rather it may stimulate more industrial conflict, but this conflict becomes one for relative advantage and is no longer motivated by the bitter revolutionary spirit that rends the community asunder and threatens the very foundations of the state. The extremity of class warfare is associated with sheer exploitation and utter insecurity, where masses of men face destitution or tyranny or both together and find no prospect but through revolt. Then they feel they have "nothing to lose but their chains". The better prospect that men have found in the life of North America, together with an actual standard of living for the most part somewhat higher than in other countries, explains quite simply the relative absence here of this revolutionary attitude. It is only in the presence of drastic conditions that men choose between drastic alternatives. Hence it is most likely that with the enhancement of economic prosperity under an established international order, when the vast powers of modern technology are devoted to constructive and no longer to destructive purposes and when liberated international trade enables every country to employ its resources to greater advantage than before, the development of extreme class war can be avoided.

There are certain things that nearly all human beings feel the need of, in such a way that when they are totally deprived of these things their allegiance to the social order is destroyed and they are ready, given any opportunity, to overthrow it; while if they obtain any measure of satisfaction of these needs they continue to struggle within the social order, but not consciously against it. Men need a degree of economic security and some kind of status in the society to which they belong. It is the thwarting of their need in one or other or both of these respects that evokes in them the spirit of revolution. This fact is easily confirmed by the study of revolutionary movements. The explanation, for example, of the role played by Jewish intellectuals in modern revolutionary movements is that these men of high endowments have been the victims of racial prejudice, have been subjected to disesteem and discrimination, and have been so wounded in their personal dignity and in their social feelings that they were filled with resentment against the social order under which they suffered. It is a curious reflection that they have thus been spurred by essentially non-economic motives to support a creed one of the main tenets of which is that economic factors are always the determinants of social revolution.

Considerations of this kind confirm the importance we have attached, in the structure of the international order, to the greater charter guaranteeing the cultural and social integrity of minority groups. But we are here considering more particularly the matter of economic insecurity. The general increase of economic prosperity accompanying the international order will not suffice of itself to remove this most serious, pervasive, and deep-working evil of modern industrial life. All industrialized states have been compelled to take measures to mitigate it, and the compulsion will not cease but rather will become stronger. The populations that at the call of their countries have offered everything in war will certainly demand to be protected in peace from this fatal insecurity. Regardless of what political parties may come into power, this demand is certain, one way or another, sooner or later, to be met. The great interest aroused everywhere by the Beveridge Report on social security in Britain is a sign of the times, and still more of the times to come.

The development of social security raises its own problems, but if we can meet the problems of war we can surely meet the far less exacting problems of peace. In every human advance there is the hazard of excess over against the hazard of defect. The former may need to be guarded against, but certainly not by refusing to remove the latter. With modern industrial productivity and the prevailing birth rates there can be no reasonable objection and no genuine economic obstacle to the necessary protection against the social insecurity that accompanies these modern conditions. There is nothing utopian about the provision of a decent minimum for all, about insurance against the economic consequences of unemployment and ill-health. In areas where the life, health, and decent living of men are at stake, the operation of the profit motive cannot be allowed to determine economic conditions. It is profitable to society as a whole that all physically capable persons be supplied with work to do, and since there is no lack on the one hand of useful work to be done or on the other hand of the food and other necessities for their maintenance, the only problem that remains is a technical one—that of devising the best system for the achievement of this objective. There are foolish expedients and there are wise ones, but the need is such and the trend of events is such that everywhere, sooner or later, some way will be found.

It lies beyond the scope of this book to enter on these questions. For this present survey it suffices that modern states are clearly oriented towards programs of greatly extended social security. Whatever more this prospect offers, it certainly reduces the probability of internal revolutions such as might seriously injure or even wreck the greater law. In fact we may sum up the matter by claiming that among the benefits the International Confederation will bring to mankind will be the enhanced stability of all the member states and thus the permanence of its own realm of peace.

Given social security and the protection of minority groups against exploitation and gross discrimination, no important element of society will be disposed to revolutionary activities. Men become revolutionists only when the iron has entered their souls. In this sense it may be claimed that revolutions are always justified, that the blame must rest on the established order rather than on those who revolt against it. The best proof that a social order is based on equity is that no considerable group of men are minded to overthrow it by violence. When the laboring population is secured against the great menaces of unemployment and destitution it no longer thinks of itself as a proletariat fighting a war to the end against a bourgeoisie. Secure labor has a quite different spirit. In fact it tends to the other extreme and is likely to join with the employing interests in seeking monopolistic advantages and in furthering price policies, tariff policies, and so forth, that increase the relative gains of the industry at the expense of the consumer.

Under these conditions we see no longer the embattled front of irreconcilable forces engaged in the life-and-death struggle of class war. Instead we see the confused strife of many groups, each seeking relative dominance and economic advantage but nevertheless all bound together by common interests and inclusive loyalties. In place of a great dividing line, on one side of which stand the upholders of the existing order while on the other are ranged those who would overthrow it altogether, we see many criss-crossing lines and many partial and shifting conflicts; the fluctuating gains and losses of entrepreneur groups, labor groups, agricultural groups, public service groups, and so forth, within a system that increases the gains and minimizes the losses of them all. We see everywhere special interests, within as well as between the greater groups. We see everywhere the tendencies of interests to entrench themselves (and we see it not least in government itself, where a bureaucracy in spite of internal divisions forever seeks to maintain ascendancy) but everywhere we see these entrenchments yielding to inevitable change and the accumulative resistance of other interests.

To such struggle there is no end. And beyond such struggle there are other struggles without end. There is no panacea in peace. No settlement settles things. Crises will occur, and then new crises, and the problem of government is never solved.

New discoveries, new disturbances, new aspirations, the constant surge of the new and the constant crumbling of the old—these things will not cease. The relation of man to man, of group to group, of people to people, are perplexedly changeful. But this also we can see: that under the greater law the promise of change will be brighter and the threat of it less dreadful. For now these crises and disturbances will fulfil themselves in less futile and less devastating ways than that of war; they will find their outlet in other operations than the sheer brutality of world-wide ruin. Man has traveled far in an amazingly short stretch of time. Civilized man lives on a level that a few thousand years ago was beyond the wildest dream. To reach it he has had to solve many problems. Ours are not the problems of the past nor those of the future; our problem belongs peculiarly to the present, that of creating some kind of international order, some kind of abiding peace.

CHAPTER TWELVE

DEMOCRACY AND THE FUTURE

I

SOME one is always making afresh the discovery that democracy is dead or dying. It is not Mussolini and his Fascists alone who cry their war chants over the decomposing corpse. It is not Hitler and his Nazis alone who pronounce democracy effete and outmoded—though in the next breath they claim to have created the truest and highest form of it. Some of the most respectable anti-Nazis have made similar discoveries. There are those who foresee technocrats in the seats of legislators. There are those who believe the "managerial revolution" will take over the state. There are those who think we need not parliaments but economic syndicates. There are those who think that economic power has overridden and nullified democratic forms. There are those who claim that democracy flouts the biological law of the "survival of the fittest" and is consequently headed towards perdition. There are those to whom has been revealed the "iron law of oligarchy", proving with inexorable logic that since leaders are always by nature oligarchs democracy is impossible. And there are those who have found that democracy cannot work, because the average man hasn't the time, competence, training, or knowledge to run so complicated a machine as the modern state.

The powers against which we fight have a deadly hatred of democracy. They hate its ideals and they hate its institutions. Wherever they have prevailed they have destroyed democracy. If they should triumph they would seek to root it out over all the earth. At such a time it is essential, for our programs of reconstruction, that we clarify our notions concerning the nature of democracy. At such a time it is vital, for the sustaining and strengthening of our arms, that we rid ourselves of confused and illusory interpretations of it, so that our cause stands out clear and strong and worthy of all our efforts for its sake. Our great dynamic comes from our faith. Without it we are at the mercy of every dividing interest. With it we have the strength that moves mountains.

Many of us are confused about the meaning of democracy. Sometimes we attribute to it imaginary virtues and expect from it impossible results. Sometimes we think of it as the rule of the people in a sense in which the people never actually rule. Sometimes we think of it as conferring all-round equality on all men in a way in which men are never actually equal. There are many conflicting voices about democracy. There is no small amount of foolish talk about it. Yet if we look at the states that by general agreement are named democratic, in contrast to states that are not so named, we can arrive at the meaning of democracy without too much difficulty.

Since the fifth century B.C. men have taken the name "democracy" and applied it to a certain type of political system. They have disagreed about its features and still more about its merits. But there has been no serious disagreement concerning the broad type of political system to which the name belongs. It has generally been attached to states in which a fairly inclusive citizen body elected its rulers or leaders by choosing between opposing candidates, after free discussion of their respective proposals or qualifications for office. The more inclusive the citizen body that participated in these activities the more democratic was the state. The system named democracy could be realized in greater or less degree. But whenever, on the coasts of Greece or in the valleys of Switzerland, among Germanic tribes or in medieval cities, in England, France, or the United States, in China or in India, citizens or subjects have demanded a voice in the affairs of state, wherever they have resisted controls imposed on them from above, wherever they have refused to be taxed without being represented, wherever they have claimed the right to criticize the policies of those who governed them, wherever they have developed an articulate and responsible public opinion, there, according to universal usage, the movement has been named democratic.

So, when the question is raised, we can all point at democracy, for we all recognize certain signs that denote its presence. Is this enough? Have we thereby defined it, proclaimed its meaning? By no means. We all recognize a dog when we see one, but were we asked to define dog we might be quite perplexed. It is not important for anyone except a zoologist to be able to define dog; but it is quite important, for all of us as citizens, to be able to define democracy. People are not likely to come along and, pointing out to us some strange animal that exhibits no canine features, insist that it is a dog. Nor would it much matter if they did. But people do come along and, pointing to some strange-looking form of government that to us reveals no democratic aspects, declare passionately that it is a democracy or indeed the true democracy. Even Adolf Hitler has done this. Similarly people come along and tell us what "real" liberty is, pointing to something that to our bewildered eyes has a mighty resemblance to tyranny.

There is an intellectual reason for defining things, and there is sometimes, as in this instance, a practical reason. When a thing has value for us, whether it be economic value, like that of precious stones, or spiritual value, like that of the liberty of thought, we do not want to be deceived by specious claims or false resemblances. Gold would lose its value if we identified it with pyrites. The value of democracy is maintained by the difference between it and its alternatives. If we defend democracy we do so not because it is free from defects or in itself an ideal or absolute thing, but because we find it more desirable than any practicable alternatives. What has this political system to offer that the others lack? What does it lack that the others

offer? Often, because we do not define at all or because we
define badly, the alternatives are not fairly stated. For example,
the alternatives are not, as many apologists have claimed, the
rule of the many and the rule of "the best". As though nature
or art offered us these alternatives! If people do not choose
their rulers what alternative method of choice sets "the best"
on the throne? Again, the alternatives are not the rule of "the
mass" and the rule of the few. The mass, in the sense of Ortega
y Gasset, has effective unity only when the social organization is shaken by a major crisis. It is the crowd swollen to national dimensions, breaking the bounds of organized life. And
when that happens the mass demands not democracy but its
Führer. The opportunity is provided for dictatorship. For then
the Leader can become the Pied Piper, playing such cunning
notes on his propaganda pipes that he leads men whither he wills.

These pseudo-alternatives take many forms. We are told, for
example, that democracy is incompatible with socio-economic
planning, whereas planning is of the very essence of dictatorship. Neither part of the statement is in accord with the facts.
Dictatorship offers us a quickly constructed and quickly executed plan of some sort, superimposed and shielded from criticism. Democracy offers us the kind and degree of planning that
public opinion will support, always subject to the criticism of
opposing forces. Dictatorship includes the cultural life in its
planning range. Democracy is incompatible with the direct control of the cultural life. These differences by no means sum up
to the contrast between a planned order and an unplanned drift.
Nor do they imply that the scheme of order in a dictatorship
is more stable or more secure than in a democracy, or even that
a dictatorship solves the problem of a crisis more completely
than does a democracy. Dictatorships arise during grave crises
because they are congenial to distracted or desperate men,
perhaps because under bad conditions better government can
not be achieved.

When we look at democracy in the light of its alternatives

its meaning is not far from us. What does it offer us that no alternative can provide? The answer is not a matter of opinion but of fact. It is written in the record. Democracy is the only political scheme that makes government constitutionally responsive to the free tides of public opinion. Its constitution is the only one that rests on the right of all citizens to have an opinion about their government and to organize that opinion so that they determine, or at least control, the policies of government. It is the sole political scheme that allows men to differ freely in opinion, drawing the line, if at all, only at the point where groups threaten to establish a system that would deny the same right to others. Democracy is the only political scheme that is inherently precluded from the direct control of the faiths, the aspirations, the life principles of its citizens, and that must leave culture free to follow its own creative way. For it could not control the motions of culture without repudiating the primary right of opinion. Finally, democracy is the only political system that makes the state the changing ever-responsive agency of the community, instead of imposing on the community the sheer stamp of the state.

Whatever organization, planning, direction, leadership, may be compatible with these principles, democracy admits; whatever is incompatible with them, democracy rejects. We have defined democracy as the institutional embodiment of certain principles. We have not defined it as being any particular set of institutions, nor on the other hand have we defined it as being merely a set of principles. We do not identify it with a parliamentary system or a representative system or any sort of economic system or any specific mechanism of government, no matter how closely associated with the history of democracy. These systems change; they must change if they are to adapt themselves to changing conditions and to changing needs. Why, for example, should we imagine that a senate and a house of representatives constitute the eternal sacred form in which the public business of a democratic society must be transacted?

They were created to meet a situation that was not sacred and is certainly not eternal. Still less do we identify democracy with majority-rule. That would be a loose and utterly misleading identification, since a majority can crush the democratic rights of a minority and give itself up to dictatorship. On the other hand we do not identify democracy with unembodied principles, such as the self-realization of a people, the solidarity of the nation, or the liberty of the individual. Vague principles of this sort provide no clear ground for distinguishing democracy from alternative political schemes, and indeed the proponents of these opposing schemes often proclaim that they satisfy these principles better than does democracy. We can find no criterion of democracy in principles without institutional embodiment or in institutions apart from principles.

The meaning of democracy is given in the relation of the two. Democracy abides wherever political institutions ensure the free role of a public opinion that extends its own freedom into the future. Therein lies the freedom of a people, the freedom of its unity, and the freedom of the differences within it. Those who believe in democracy know that with this double freedom human life achieves a dignity and a creative power that all other systems deny.

2

With the other foolish things said against democracy by its enemies goes the contention that it is outdated, that it belonged to a particular historical phase now ended, and that it is out of harmony with modern conditions and modern needs. It is thought of as an aspect of the "liberalistic nineteenth century", and the "liberalism" is supposed to have died with the century. Modern technology, modern heavy industry, the economic corporation and the cartel, the organization of labor, of agriculture, of all other large-scale interests, with the consequent collectivism imposed on the state, have changed the problem of government. Democracy is no longer the solution.

The problems of government have changed, but the ultimate problem of government remains and cannot but remain the same. It is the problem of what the historian Ferrero has called its legitimacy. No form of government, anywhere or in any age, has been enduring that has not rested on the consent of the people of the primary land over which the government rules. This consent has been derived from two different sources. One is the tradition of the people, inclining them to accept some authority hallowed by religion and by custom. Usually, though not always, this type of authority is monarchical. The other is the active participation of the people, under constitutional forms, as a result of which they set up, and change from time to time, the government favored by the majority or plurality vote. This is the democratic type.

Now under modern conditions the traditional type of legitimacy is less likely to prevail. Custom is no longer unified. A country has seldom one religion. Groups and interests are diverse and conflicting. The people are less apt to be content with passive acquiescence in pre-established authority. They demand control over the power that rules them. Under such conditions the only source of legitimacy is democratic participation. The traditional type of legitimacy is characteristic of simpler conditions. In that sense it is more primitive. The democratic type is characteristic of complex civilization. In that sense it is more evolved. But always the choice lies between one or the other—unless we find some combination of the two.

Without legitimacy, however derived, government is precarious, unstable, lacking in assurance. It is a continuing *coup d'état*. It survives by force and cunning. It has no compass and no destination. It is outwardly brutal and inwardly trembling. It creates violence and counterviolence everywhere. Because it is illegitimate it is afraid of the people and establishes a terror with its spies and informers and secret police. It clothes itself in lies and pretensions to cover its naked usurpation, but no matter how clever its ideologies they cannot hide the truth.

The usurper is well aware of this and is always driven to fresh violence. At length, lest his violence turn on himself, he commits his people to the ultimate violence of war.

This illegitimate thing, this dictatorship, begotten of violence and nurtured by fear, is what its prophets proclaim to be the successor of outmoded democracy. Forms pass, but principles endure and engender new forms. The principle of legitimacy is permanent, as old as history and as new as human nature. This principle dictatorship does not satisfy, and therefore dictatorship cannot endure.

There is tragicomedy in its claim on the future. Government is no better and no wiser than those who govern. They are human beings with all the frailties of mortality and subject to all the temptations of power. They speak from on high for all to hear, and their folly or their wisdom cannot be long concealed. Their power corrupts whatever wisdom they once possessed. Where legitimacy derives from tradition the ruler, in his folly or his wisdom, is limited within the bounds of custom. Where legitimacy derives from popular election the ruler, in his folly or his wisdom, is held to account by public opinion. But dictatorship offers no safeguard either way. Yet it must, and for the very same reasons, make inordinate claims. The Führer is the gift of God to His chosen people. The Duce is "the man who incarnates the virtues of the race". The dictator, unlimited by legitimacy, must be unlimited in wisdom; he must be eternally right. The exposure is inevitable at length. The superlative claims become ludicrous, grotesque. The Duce becomes a mountebank, the Führer a blind driver to the pit.

Let us hear some of the words of wisdom spoken by the biggest of the dictators. This man, who before every act of aggression proclaimed that he sought nothing but to live at peace with the world, announced the declaration of war with the United States as follows: "An historic revenge has been entrusted to us by the Creator, and we are now bound to carry it out." He went on to explain that the American President was not only "totally incompetent" but also addicted to malpractice in business. "In fact, in Europe it seems inconceivable that Roosevelt should not have ended before a state court. In fact he would presumably, before a civil court, have received a term of imprisonment for sharp practice in business." He concluded the argument thus: "I consider President Roosevelt to be insane. . . . We know, of course, that the eternal Jew is behind all this. . . . Indeed, we all know the intention of the Jews to rule all civilized states in Europe and America."

So spoke the Infallible One, He-Who-Is-Always-Right. When he said it, twelve European states lay at his heel. In all these states no man dared, on pain of death, to express aloud any opinion that doubted his sacred word. This system of government, this dictatorship, this elevation of brute power above all human rights and decencies, is the system, so we are told, that owns the future. By violence and fear it rules its hour. Precarious and illegitimate, it seeks to maintain itself by war. And at length by war, in the midst of the widespread ruin it has made, it perishes.

No government can endure unless it is, or becomes, legitimate. Of the two forms of legitimacy the democratic, where the conditions admit it, has certain great advantages. Indeed these advantages are so great that it can reasonably claim the future, provided civilization continues to advance and the vigor of culture does not decay.

Democracy, to speak first of its pre-eminent advantage, is the only system of government that reconciles political order with political liberty. All governments establish order of some kind; non-democratic governments establish it at the cost of certain fundamental liberties; democratic government establishes it on the basis of these same liberties. These liberties are as follows:

(1) A series of liberties, often called *civil liberties*, dependent on restraint of the executive and administrative agencies of government. In a democracy the executive must act under laws it is not free to make or to break. Hence liberties are enjoyed

against such things as arbitrary arrest, imprisonment without trial, trial without legal guarantees, sentence without right of appeal, and other acts of discrimination or oppression by particular agents of the government.

(2) A series of liberties, often called *constitutional liberties*, dependent on restraint of the lawmaking organ, so that it is denied the right to do certain things, such as to make any law respecting an establishment of religion or abridging the freedom of speech or of the press. These are the liberties embodied in the Bill of Rights. In nearly all democracies they are defined in a written constitution, though in the democracy of Great Britain they are guarded simply by the effective power of the democratic spirit.

(3) A series of liberties, which for the sake of distinction we shall call *public liberties*, dependent on the right of the people to elect their own government, in accordance with the changing trends of public opinion. Here is included the liberty to vote, the liberty to belong to a political party, the liberty to stand for office, and so forth. These are the liberties of political action, and they reinforce and in turn are buttressed by the liberties belonging to the first and second series.

Such are the democratic liberties that are bound up with democratic order. They are not perfectly assured in our democracies, but that is because democracy is itself imperfect. To assure them better we need better democracy. No alternative system of government assures them at all; dictatorship crushes them altogether. These liberties do not cover all the liberties that men prize, and there are other things besides their liberties that men prize. There are many other things without which their democratic liberties may seem to them formal and rather empty. But these considerations do not diminish the primary worth of democratic liberties as the safeguard of human dignity and the condition of creative adventure throughout the whole realm of human values. Nor should they hide the fact that these same liberties are a most potent means whereby men may attain many other goods they prize.

This last point needs special attention in these times. There is a tendency in some quarters—as part of the revulsion from nineteenth century liberalism—to decry democratic liberties as unimportant by the side of certain economic liberties. There is a suggestion that these economic liberties can be attained without regard for democratic liberties or even in the absence of democratic liberties. There is a claim that democracy has failed because it has not provided these economic liberties. Thus, for example, the author of *Conditions of Peace*, Mr. E. H. Carr, writes that "during the past fifty years democratic forms and political rights have been gradually emptied of their significance, even in some of the most advanced democratic countries, by the over-riding force of economic power. . . . Political rights have come to seem irrelevant in so far as they no longer confer control over those factors which determine the decisive issues of national life." While statements of this kind properly lay stress on the central problem of democracy, the manner in which they are made is very apt to mislead us with regard to the relation between democratic liberties and economic controls.

To deal at all adequately with this most challenging and difficult problem demands an analysis that would carry us too far beyond the focus and the purpose of this book. We shall confine ourselves to a few summary statements intended to show that the only hopeful and forward-looking way of meeting economic issues in the national life is the democratic way.

In the first place we deny the too sweeping assertion that in more recent times democracy has increasingly lost its efficacy because of the increasing power of organized economic interests. It can fairly be said on the other side that only in recent times has democracy been learning how to curb various forms of economic exploitation. The development of social security and public welfare programs in all modern states affords the best illustration. This development has on the whole been responsive to the political power of the people. And it is highly probable that the process is far from being at its end. Against other forms of economic exploitation, especially those practised by cartels, combines, and monopolies, less success has been achieved. The modern economic corporation has brought about, over large sections of industry and of finance, a virtual separation of control from ownership and has thus achieved an extraordinary concentration of economic power and sharpened the issue between economic power and political power. It has been shown by Berle and Means (*The Modern Corporation and Private Property*) that two hundred of the largest corporations in the United States control more than thirty-eight per cent of all business wealth and over twenty per cent of the total national wealth. The political regulation of this immensely concentrated economic power may well be the greatest and the most difficult of all the internal problems that democracy has to face. Profit-seeking capital is always resorting to new ingenious devices, and the techniques of political control always lag behind. Nevertheless, no one who is aware of the progress made in the regulation of banks, transportation systems, public utilities, and other monopolies can properly claim that political rights have been emptied of economic significance. Nor should we forget that the great exposures of unbridled economic power have been very largely due to commissions and boards of inquiry set up by democratic governments. If then there are still some very important areas of economic exploitation—and among them may be included the dictatorial powers wielded by certain highly consolidated labor interests—this fact is no ground for denying the considerable achievements of democracy or for doubting its capacity, in so far as democracy itself is alert, of winning further and more complete conquests.

In the second place the partial failure of democracy in this struggle should convey no suggestion that greater success is attainable under some alternative system of government. Two rather different schools have proposed an alternative—though each of them sometimes claims that its program is not opposed to but is rather the fulfilment of democracy. One of these alternatives is the syndicalist or corporative system, a governing organization of economic guilds being substituted for a parliament of representatives chosen without specific reference to their economic or "functional" qualifications. Under this system the central governing body would be a mosaic of representation from the organizations of agriculture, labor, business, the professions, the technicians, and so forth. Since, however, the trouble with legislators elected as presumptive representatives of the public at large is that they are apt to be swayed by their own private interests or by those of dominant groups or lobbies there is small enough reason to suppose that this corporative assembly would be more solicitous for the general weal and more ready or more able to curb the excesses of economic power.

The weakness of democracy is that in bestowing on all groups the right to organize and freely to pursue their special interests it must still trust the citizens as a whole to set the common welfare above their liberated interests. It is weak where men, seduced by private advantage, fail to justify the larger trust reposed in them. The higher system makes the higher demands. Hence a democracy must seek by all means to strengthen in the people the sense of common interest. It must seek to equalize opportunity when it confers equality of voting power. It must see to it that the common good, that in which we all share alike, is great enough to claim and to deserve the common devotion. As against all special interests the state itself must somehow be the guardian of the whole. It would therefore seem particularly unwise to make the central agency of government a body elected and organized on the basis of the specific interests or "functions" of its various members.

The other alternative is a system that transfers all major economic powers to the state itself. We speak of it as an alternative to democracy because its champions are often curiously ambivalent with respect to democracy. They say, for example: "We must socialize the means of production. Regulation is not enough." But it is reasonably clear that in most industrialized countries at the present time the wholesale socialization of the means of production could not be carried through under democratic auspices. Too considerable a proportion of the people are irremediably committed to the retention of private enterprise. Even if a majority could be obtained in support of complete socialization the resistance of the minority would be so formidable that the state would be cleft asunder. Furthermore, it is extremely doubtful, to say the least, whether a completely socialized state could under any conditions retain a democratic character. So many everyday affairs would have to be regulated by authority; so many decisions concerning occupation, income, the price of commodities, and so forth, would have to be centrally determined: so many matters now in the realm of style and taste and preference would have to be coordinated and controlled by government; so many people and so many things would have to be kept in their appointed places against all the impulses of variant desires that nothing short of the awe-invested dictator could be expected to maintain the system.

All industrialized states, since the middle of the nineteenth century, have been increasing the area of socialization. This trend has been compatible with democracy because it has been gradual, because as it moved it established new habituations, because it still left room and to spare for the individualistic impulses. The process is not fulfilled. It may advance considerably further. But this advancing process of socialization, with its give-and-take, with its experimentation, with its continuous readjustment of existing relationships and forces, is a very different thing from the drastic substitution of political for economic power that the proponents of complete state socialism demand.

These proponents say again: "Political democracy is not

enough. We must have economic democracy." But the language is misleading. If they mean that democracy must take measures to restrain economic power, to curb economic exploitation, to broaden economic opportunity, to provide economic security, that is one thing; but that is *political* democracy in action. If they mean, as their language suggests, that besides political democracy there is another—and superior—kind called economic democracy, that is confused thinking. When it comes to the regulation of economic affairs there is one kind of democracy, and one only. All governments regulate economic affairs; democratic governments regulate them by democratic processes. These processes can be improved, policies and objectives can be revised, new and better controls can be set up—but it is still political democracy that operates in all this. And what it thus achieves is the greater economic well-being of the people, *but not economic democracy*. And complete state socialism has certainly no better claim to be called economic democracy than has any other system. Indeed, as we have just been pointing out, there is a serious danger that under it political democracy, the only form of democracy that has meaning on the national scale, may suffer shipwreck.

So we return to our conclusion that the only hopeful and forward-looking way of meeting the challenge of economic power is that which democracy offers. To this we now add our final point, that democracy is far better able than any alternative system to hold in subjection another form of power, one that more directly menaces the international order. We refer to the power of the military, in so far as that power intrudes into the political sphere. In this respect the record of democracy is clear and convincing. Both the spirit of democracy and the constitutional relation it establishes between the legislative and the executive organs, subjecting the latter to the control of the former, tend to divest the military of political authority. By and large, democratic policies are not deflected by any general staff, any officers' corps, any military caste. This fact is amply revealed in the history of England, the United States, the Scandinavian countries, Switzerland, the British Dominions, and democratic countries as a whole. Whereas in non-democratic countries military leadership is nearly always influential in politics, and not infrequently, as in modern Germany, it has been in the ascendant.

This fact holds also an omen for the future of democracy. It is where states are insecure that the political power of the military is apt to be most decisive. In the international order that is coming, sooner or later, states will attain, for reasons on which we have already dwelt, a new security. In the same order the military arm will be in effect abolished, or reduced to such small proportions as to make it politically negligible. Thus one of the chief factors making against a democratic regime will disappear. We cannot, in the present state of the world, build our international order on democratic states alone. But should we succeed in building this international order we shall at the same time be preparing a greater future for democracy.

CHAPTER THIRTEEN

THE PECULIAR ROLE OF THE UNITED STATES

I

THOSE who pay the piper like to call the tune. The heaviest brunt of this vastest of all wars has not been borne by the United States. Without the direct and the indirect participation of the United States, without its final massing of economic and military strength, a clean-cut victory of the allied powers would have remained a most dubious prospect. (This statement has of course nothing to do with the stupid and mischief-making question as between allies: "Who won the war?") At the same time it is true that the brute weight of the conflict was carried first by Britain, in the lone days of its splendid resistance, and next by Russia, in the consuming fury of desperate battle and magnificent resurgence over the enormous Eastern front. Any program of settlement must meet the main demands of the governments of these countries. Happily, in spite of their extreme diversity in cultural background and in economic philosophy, these two powers are at one in their realistic will for an international order, and they are both pledged to a settlement that, so far as international issues are concerned, is broadly in accord with the principle of democracy. On the whole their divergences from this principle, on the one hand the aristocratic-imperialistic heritage of Britain, so far as it still remains influential, on the other hand the proletarian assumptions of Soviet Russia, are in opposite directions. Between these opposites stands the United States. This situation is the first of the conditions on which depends the peculiar and profoundly significant role of the United States.

Furthermore, the United States is not entangled in the contentions and historical divisions that have embroiled Europe and brought it to despair and ruin. Within its own receptive nationality it has, through the favor of geography, fortune, and the Constitution, taken the immigrants from European countries and united them in a citizenship that transcends ethnic divisions. While it has still to overcome some of the socio-economic problems of interethnic assimilation it has effectively met the political problem. So far as its European stocks are concerned it has no memories of ethnic hatreds, no legacies of ethnic feuds. Its scheme of government is in essentials undisturbed by the religious and cultural differences of its people. On the whole it has created an American way of life that has embraced in a common tradition the heterogeneity of its component groups. The United States is not alone in this respect. It is the contribution of the American continent. Under a different flag a similar fusion has been achieved over the greater part of the Dominion of Canada. In one form or another it has been developing over the whole of the Western hemisphere.

Because it is thus liberated from the divisions that beset Europe, because it has been the traditional land of opportunity and asylum for the oppressed, because it is a republic as well as a democracy, because it is the greatest of genuinely federal unions, the peoples of Continental Europe see in the United States the realistic answer to many of their own problems. To them, to the masses at least, the United States of America, viewed from across the ocean, offers a shining example. They have looked to it for leadership, and in spite of the great disillusionment they experienced after the First World War, they are still disposed to be responsive to its leadership.

There is of course the further very important consideration that while all the other great countries have been economically exhausted or at the least impoverished by the war the United States retains and has indeed augmented its vast economic strength. It has expended astronomical sums, it has taxed its people beyond previous conception, it has incurred great new obligations, through its national debt, through its commitments to its veterans and its fallen, and through the coming necessity of retransforming a total war economy into one geared to the demands of peace. But these obligations do not impair its economic strength. What the state owes the people own. What the state distributes the people possess. The country has escaped the direct ravage of war as no other among the major belligerents has done. Without causing any serious hardship to its own people it has supplied immense quantities of foodstuffs and other goods to its allies all over the world. It has provided them with more armament power than was ever mustered by both sides in any previous war. It has at the same time fed and clothed and equipped its own tremendous air force and navy and army. And if there is truth in the ancient saying that money is the sinews of war, there is also truth in the addendum that money is the sinews of reconstruction. The primary economic tasks of reconstruction, the rehabilitation of devastated areas and the relief of starving peoples, the financing necessary to re-establish stricken industries, the re-opening of trade channels, the setting up of an international bank and credit system—in sum, the whole vast difficult business of restoring, confirming, and advancing a peacetime economy, to bring a new prospect of prosperity to the whole world, including the United States, depends on the statesmanship of this country. The world recognizes this fact, and this fact alone is enough to give the United States its grandest and most profoundly challenging opportunity for leadership.

The historic moment calls. The tide in the affairs of men nears the flood. If we take it we set the world an example more resounding, we bring to it a guidance even more resplendent, than was revealed at the founding of this Republic. If we miss it, if we reject this second opportunity within the space of two generations, this clearer and more decisive opportunity, it will pass from our grasp and the future will be shaped by other peoples, after long tribulation and turmoil that we could have stayed, after renewed sorrows that we could have ended.

There is grave danger that we shall fail the world. It is ready for us. We may be unready for it. Although we enjoy at this time a position of peculiar advantage, we are baulked by moral unreadiness, by the gross persistence of parochial attitudes in the hour of destiny. These may paralyze our statesmenship. There is grave danger that we shall lose the peace.

Bestriding a continent, our people find it hard to think in terms of the world. The most multigroup of nations, they find it hard to think in terms of their own unity, their common cause. They believe in their unity; they have faith in an "American way of life". But they are at a loss to give it conscious expression. They shy away from the attempt, and their intellectual leaders rarely help them. Our people take their unity for granted, and turn their thoughts to other issues, mostly to the issues that divide them. But there are times when a people must be conscious of what it has achieved, of what it stands for, of what it needs to achieve. It is more difficult for a democratically minded people to do so, but sometimes, for the sake of its very democracy, it is imperative. Now, with the future of the world in the balance, is one of these historic times.

For reasons in part creditable, this people was slow to achieve its unity in a world at war. Once the decision was forced upon it, it hesitated no more. Differences and difficulties were swept aside in the intense and triumphant concentration on arms. But this common cause, though paramount, remains nevertheless external, defensive, directed against a peril but not oriented towards a goal. This common cause is pursued with costly and devoted efficiency, but with little regard to positive ends beyond the deliverance of victory itself. The sense of national unity sustains the common devotion, even though it remains inarticulate. But while that may suffice for the winning of victory, it will not suffice for the reaping of its fruits. Unless the conception of a goal beyond victory is realized, unless it is given clear strong authoritative utterance, unless it becomes dynamic in the mind as well as in the heart of the people, from all our toils and sacrifices no constructive gain will come, no positive good for ourselves and for the world.

It is folly to say: "Let us first win the war and then attend to these things—if we now raise the issues of the peace, except in fine round phrases, we shall engender divisions, distract our energies, and create difficulties between ourselves and our allies." Having already dealt with this folly we shall here be content to reply that preparation is everything, for peace as well as for war. Nor is it enough to leave to our leaders the preparation for peace while the rest of us forget about it. Of all countries the United States can least afford to follow that prescription. When the time for the making of peace has come, we shall be helpless without the aroused and enlightened opinion of the people. There are certain features of the social and political life of this country that constitute a peculiar danger to our effectiveness in peacemaking, as they did also at the end of the First World War.

Unless we make preparation in the time of war, when the sense of national unity is heightened, when our private concerns are subordinated or in abeyance, when we are more ready for larger purposes and greater achievements, then the ringing of the bells of peace will be the signal for our return to our narrower ways, to our heterogeneous groups, to our dividing interests. We shall speedily say farewell to all that. The consciousness of our unity will again be dissipated, for it will no longer be upheld by the sense of any common end still to be fulfilled. We shall miss the flood tide. We shall remain grounded in the shallows, when the world's need, which is our own as well, calls us to greater adventure and greater achievement.

After war comes the reaction. Men yearn for the near familiar things. They want to forget the tension and the strain. They want to have a good time at last—and it is perfectly natural, perfectly understandable that they should. But under these conditions they will advance no far-sighted plans. They will be ready for "normalcy". They will be more inclined than before to cherish the illusions of isolationism. The lesson of two world wars, that isolation is no longer possible, that no seas can separate us from the beat of world affairs, will be forgotten. The eternal noises of European dissensions, the confused strife that will still rage over its wasted starving lands, will make us thank God to be out of it. We shall devoutly hang the musket on the wall and go about "our own affairs". And these tendencies will be diligently fostered by those who have their own axes to grind.

Unless public opinion is stirred and educated in advance the coming of peace will find us unprepared, and if the people is unprepared our best statesmanship, for reasons peculiar to this republic, will be ineffective. When we speak here of "public opinion" and "the people" we are not under any delusion that the people is ever a unity on any question of policy, and we are not attributing to public opinion any superior wisdom. We mean merely that the people will be in sufficient volume responsive to its common interest if that interest is made plain. We mean that it will in sufficient volume resist the specious pleas of narrower interests if it is aroused to the greater need. We mean that in the time of war, when its consciousness of that need is heightened, it will be more responsive than in the relaxation that comes with peace. We mean that the momentum of public opinion that can be engendered in the day of war will in sufficient measure carry through to the day of peace. We do not expect that the people will then embark on some great crusade. Let them have their good time, so far as they can. Let them have, so far as they can, the relaxation that is due after great efforts and sacrifices. Let our fighters, and our workers too, enjoy at length a greater fullness of living. But that better time need not be less good because men have intelligent attitudes towards the future. It need not be impaired because they vote for leaders who share these attitudes. It is not affected because they support policies that will save their children from the blasting flame of war. They can still hang the musket on the wall and go about their own affairs.

The grave danger is that the sense of national unity evoked by war will be dissipated by peace, and with it the recognition of national need and of national opportunity. The tendency will be for specific interests to dominate and for the inclusive interest to be lost from sight. The divisions of domestic politics are likely to become all engrossing and between them to stultify and distract our international program. The struggle for economic and political advantage, spreading through local, regional, state, and federal arenas, will fetter the activities of our statesmen when they must assume their most difficult and momentous task. It is the peril of our system, of our multiform and crazy-quilt democracy, that it does not suffer us to separate local from national, domestic from international issues. The spoils of office are so tempting and affect so large a number that national considerations are often at the mercy of the lower conflicts for place and power. It is this condition that enables the caucus to put up for office men disgracefully unqualified, that gives the ward-heeler his control over the votes, that makes the party machine so powerful, that makes the primary so futile. Only when the people are thoroughly roused by some great call to action can this peril be overcome.

Otherwise little men and selfish interests will have their way, oblivious of the nation's greatness, regardless of the nation's task. Working with them will be everywhere the tariff booster. He will distort the issues. He will masquerade as a patriot. Having already his large market he will endeavor to shut out others who have smaller markets, and he will adduce his skilfully false arguments to delude the people. Ignorant even of his own long-run good he will seek to harm the good of all others. Not knowing what he does, he will menace the international order that needs to be born. And many will believe his words.

The danger of divisive interests runs from the bottom to the top of the political pyramid. Of the powers that will write the terms of peace the United States alone runs a serious risk of having divided counsels *within the system of the government itself*. The United States alone suffers the additional encumbrance that the international pacts made by its accredited leaders may be defeated and rejected by a minority vote in the Senate. The American scheme of government is not adjusted to the need for unity and decisiveness in foreign policy. This fact was strongly insisted upon by Woodrow Wilson many years before he himself became the outstanding victim of it. When a minister of state makes a pronouncement it is often quite uncertain whether he speaks for the government or only for himself. If, for example, the Secretary of War pens a congratulatory letter to Hapsburg Otto it remains a matter of conjecture whether this action is approved by the Department of State or by the President or by any one else in the government. Different ministers may move in opposite directions, and the ministry as a whole may be at cross purposes with the majority in the Congress—or with the veto-owning minority in the Senate. While in the actual conduct of the war these difficulties are greatly reduced by the special wartime powers vested in the President they return full force when it comes to the making of peace.

To complete the tale there is a culminating embarrassment. We know with practical certainty who will speak for England and who for Russia and who for China at the peace table. We know under what auspices the representatives of these countries will be appointed. But we do not know well ahead who will speak for the United States, we do not know what party, majority, or leader will be in control. Thus forward planning for the peace is subject to a great question mark. Certainly no one will deny that the government should mature in advance its program of reconstruction. Nor can it be doubted that the United States is at a disadvantage, compared with other states, from its inability to frame its own specific peace policies with any assurance that these will still be approved by the dominant party when the time for implementation arrives. Serious difficulties might be avoided if the government could arrive at an understanding with the allied governments on certain issues. A thorough exchange of views with Soviet Russia is, for example, eminently desirable. The situation that has developed in Yugoslavia is simply a preview of the ominous clashes and confusions that will later arise in the absence of such understandings. It may not be going too far to claim that by entering, in conjunction with Britain, into a pre-understanding with Russia—in which, while sympathetic to her needs, we stand by our own principles—we can dispel the menace of deadly civil war in Eastern Europe and elsewhere, perhaps even in China, a spreading civil war that might well blight all the prospects of the settlement.

In the light of all these conditions how bereft of insight are those who say: "Let us first win the war and then we can attend to the peace"! Only by the strong marshalling of public opinion, only by the evocation of the positive consciousness of national unity, only by the pervading recognition of what is implied in American democracy and in the peace-loving American way of life—and by the translation of that recognition into a consistent program of international policy for the benefit of all peoples, and ourselves not least—only so will it be possible for the United States to accept her mission and to fulfil her role.

2

In this country it is for the people to say; it lies with the people to prevail. The things that unite them are far greater than the things that divide. They can also be far more potent, but only if they are positively asserted in the strong consciousness of unity. The things that unite us must become dynamic in our policy. They cannot be if at this momentous juncture we think of our unity in terms of isolation. National isolationism is the evil opposite of the evil separatism that the Nazis profess, but whereas their separatism is ruthlessly aggressive our isolationism is feebly static.

The unity of a people is squandered in isolation. Just as the individual person attains his being in and through his relations with others so the nation becomes a vital whole only as it plays its part in world affairs. If it shrinks back into itself when great issues are loosed between the nations, when the future of the world is being shaped, then its unity, its integrity, is no more than the shadowy remembrance of its past. Because the United States is one of the great powers, it cannot escape the consequences of its world position, even if it seeks to evade the responsibility. It will be the victim of the world forces that it refuses to face. Its role will be determined for it by petty narrow-visioned disintegrating interests unless, in the decisive hour, it rediscovers its unity and translates it into action.

It is not at all a question of our imposing our own way on the world. It is not a question of our going forth as world missionary or as world social agency. We do not go abroad, away from ourselves, when we take our part in world concerns. They are also our concerns, for by the necessity of our nationhood we belong to the world of nations. We cannot confine our interests within our frontiers. At one time to possess our frontiers was enough for us, and the tradition of that long and arduous task still lingers in a way that obscures for many the newer and wider responsibilities that its fulfilment inevitably has thrust upon us. Now our interests carry us to the far corners of the earth. It is our own good that binds us to the good of other nations.

If we are to be worthy of our position as a world power we must first learn how to act with unity in world affairs. We can no longer permit the partisan strife of domestic politics to distract, confound, and nullify our international status. We failed, largely on that account, in 1919. We need above all to find some way to dissociate the business of peace making from party advantage. This is a difficult, complicated problem, because the stakes of party dominance concern so many interests of such diverse kinds. Only if the people are united enough to insist upon it is there any hope of its being accomplished.

In the first place the United States representation at the peace table should contain leading men from the two major parties. This procedure would require, from the party actually in control, an act of abnegation. It is not likely that in the longer run they would lose by doing so, and certainly they would lose by not doing so if public opinion can be sufficiently aroused to the need for this procedure. The exceptional political circumstances under which, for the first time in history, a President of the United States holds office for a third term give additional weight to a still more drastic proposal. On the assumption that the settlement, or any beginning of it, is to be made while Franklin Roosevelt remains president, we believe that the best or perhaps the only way to achieve the desired result would be that he forthwith renounce any further participation in domestic politics, save for the formal responsibilities of his present term of office, in order to devote himself to international affairs, and that he invite the leading personality on the Republican side, his opponent at the 1940 presidential election, to join with him as an equal partner in the ensuing negotiations.

In effect this proposal is remarkably in accord with the spirit of the Constitution. When its founders agreed upon the clause empowering the President to make treaties in conjunction with the Senate, "provided two-thirds of the senators present concur", they were seeking to ensure that the treaty-making power be as broadly based as possible—though the debates show that narrower motives were also at work. They ignored, here as elsewhere, the existence of political parties, nor could they possibly have foreseen the crucial importance that the struggle of parties would later assume. So their provision for treaty-making has come to incur the grave danger of serving a purpose that is practically the opposite of the one originally intended. It allows a minority party group to overrule for its own advantage the will of a very considerable majority. Only if both the major parties are equally implicated can we have any assurance that America's role in the great settlement will not be frustrated and rendered void by some band of dissentients.

The risk of internal disagreement in the "equal partnership" here proposed is not very serious. The two leaders in question have shown alike a realistic appreciation of America's stake in international affairs. On essentials they stand together. Together they express the dynamic spirit of America on the issues of war and peace. Where differences arise a way could be found of meeting them by reference to the larger delegation. Both leaders firmly believe in the necessity of an international order, and in the development and in the service of this order not one alone but both might seek his future—a contingency that would still more completely serve to remove from the accidents and schisms of domestic politics the profoundly important contribution of the United States to the world that is to be.

So, in unity of purpose backed by economic strength, the United States would move on to the fulfilment of its historic role. It would confirm the forces that oppose the old imperialism. It would act single-mindedly for the liberation of all peoples. It would successfully oppose the spirit of revenge that recks nothing of future good. It would, we believe, reject the militarist spirit that seeks short-lived security by such schemes as the total occupation of Germany after the armistice. It would strongly aid to establish the necessary interim governments of countries overrun by the enemy, and as strongly insist that these same countries be given the first opportunity to choose their own governments. It would powerfully discourage any projects among the allies to amass territorial gains. It would be particularly effective in making and financing plans for a new international economy. It would enthusiastically support the greater charter under which the cultural rights of all groups would be guaranteed. It would join with its neighbor Canada in showing how inviolate frontiers can be without fortifications to guard the line. It would bring with it the will for peace of a whole hemisphere, from ocean to ocean and from pole to pole. And it would throw its decisive weight in favor of the institutions of a genuine international system.

Perhaps its international vision would be too simple, too heedless of the tangled implications of tradition, too idealistic. But that very simplicity of outlook would help, not hinder, when the great powers meet as arbiters of destiny. Even where it yielded before the stubbornness of opposing realisms it would still have moved them in the direction towards which the world must move. Woodrow Wilson was accused of idealism, but that would have been his strength and not his weakness if he had not sacrificed the spirit of it to save the form. But enough has happened since 1919, and a vastly troubled world is riper for leadership.

If we are too idealistic, so long as our vision is directed to concrete applications and not to abstractions, we are likely to advance further than in any other way. The whole is never attained, but only by pursuing the whole can we make heroic gains. At the end there remains the same old earth, but there is always some new heaven. The old remains in the new, to save us from the folly of our dreams. The new emerges from the old, to save our dreams themselves. The transformation of systems, economic or political, goes on without end. What is built must always be rebuilt. The task of statesmanship is to realize the dreams that the insight of the statesman can seize upon as capable of being translated into the substance of earth.

A few passages printed in this book have already appeared in contributions of the author to the *Journal of Legal and Political Sociology*, *New Europe*, *Vital Speeches*, and the *Third Symposium* of The Conference on Science, Philosophy and Religion. They are here reprinted with permission.